****

ENGLISH PRONUNCIATION FOR SPANISH SPEAKERS: Vowels

****

PAULETTE DALE, Ph.D.

Miami-Dade Community College

LILLIAN POMS, M.Ed.

Hearing and Speech Center of Florida, Inc.

PRENTICE-HALL, INC., Englewood Cliffs, New Jersey 07632

Editorial/production supervision and interior design: Virginia Rubens
Cover design: Ben Santora
Manufacturing buyer: Harry P. Baisley

Printed in the United States of America

10   9   8   7   6   5   4   3

0-13-281312-2   01

PRENTICE-HALL INTERNATIONAL, INC., *London*
PRENTICE-HALL OF AUSTRALIA PTY. LIMITED, *Sydney*
EDITORA PRENTICE-HALL DO BRASIL, LTDA., *Rio de Janeiro*
PRENTICE-HALL CANADA, INC., *Toronto*
PRENTICE-HALL HISPANOAMERICANA, S.A., *Mexico*
PRENTICE-HALL OF INDIA PRIVATE LIMITED, *New Delhi*
PRENTICE-HALL OF JAPAN, INC., *Tokyo*
PRENTICE-HALL OF SOUTHEAST ASIA PTE. LTD, *Singapore*
WHITEHALL BOOKS LIMITED, *Wellington, New Zealand*

CONTENTS

****

***
ACKNOWLEDGMENTS
****

The authors wish to express their sincerest gratitude to the many people who have helped develop this program:

Professor Tommie Ems of the College of Lake County; Ms. Susan Epstein of the Hearing and Speech Center of Florida; the teachers who helped field-test the materials and recommended valuable improvements;

Nilda López Morgenstern of the Dade County Public Schools and Maria Trini Arias de Gómez for generously offering to translate the Study Guide into Spanish;

Professor David Gravel, Director of Broadcasting at Miami-Dade Community College, for producing the audio cassettes and for his great role as "instructor on the tape";

Allan Poms, Jerry Dale, and the rest of our families for their support and encouragement throughout;

But most important of all, we are grateful and indebted to our students, past, present, and future, for using this program, for encouraging us, and for giving us many practical suggestions to better help us meet their needs.

AUDIO CASSETTE TAPE OUTLINE

TAPE 1

AUDIO CASSETTE TAPE OUTLINE *(cont'd.)*

TAPE 2

INTRODUCTION

****

Welcome to **English Pronunciation for Spanish Speakers**. Before we begin, we'd like to discuss "foreign accents" in general. Webster's Dictionary defines *accent* as "speech habits typical of the natives of a region." SO—we **all** have accents!

You should be PROUD of having an accent. In fact, there are advantages to having one. YES, we said advantages! A foreign accent tells listeners that you speak at least **TWO** languages. That certainly puts you far ahead of a person who can speak only one language. The world would be very dull if we all sounded the same. After all, *VARIETY IS THE SPICE OF LIFE!!!*

Unfortunately, there is a disadvantage to having a foreign accent. It may hinder effective communication in your non-native language and cause you to be misunderstood. Our main goal is to help you improve your pronunciation of American English. This will enable you to clearly communicate exactly what you want to say. We will be with you throughout this book to help you along the way!

Please turn the page and continue reading. The next section is not for *teachers;* it is **especially for you!!!**

1

```
*********************************************
```
TO THE STUDENT
```
*********************************************
```

You bought **English Pronunciation for Spanish Speakers** because you feel a need to improve your ability to speak English as a second language. We know it is frustrating to have someone say, "I can't understand you because of your accent." We also know that you might be afraid to use certain words because you'll mispronounce them. Many of our students avoid words like *sheet* and *beach*. Instead they ask for a *piece* of paper and say they went to the *ocean*. We understand your feelings and want to reassure you. PLEASE DON'T WORRY! You don't have to avoid saying certain words and phrases, and you don't have to be misunderstood by other people.

English Pronunciation for Spanish Speakers: Vowels has been written especially for YOU. You will find that this program has been designed to help you overcome your particular pronunciation problems when speaking English and that it is an independent program you can use **on your own.** The manual is written in easy-to-understand terms and is accompanied by cassette tapes to help you learn to pronounce the American English vowel sounds correctly. You don't need a teacher (or speech therapist) to use this program.

The **English Pronunciation for Spanish Speakers: Vowels** manual covers the various vowels and diphthongs in the English language. Each chapter follows a specific format and contains the following sections:

Pronouncing the Sound

A simple explanation of how to pronounce the vowel and details for actual placement of the articulators (lips, tongue, etc.) are discussed.

Spanish Key Words

Spanish key words with the equivalent English vowel are provided. These give you a familiar sound with which to relate.

Possible Pronunciation Problems for the Spanish Speaker

This section explains why the vowel creates problems for you and how your pronunciation difficulties are related to specific differences between Spanish and English.

Hints

A series of rules to help you remember when to produce the sound are provided. They will help you use English spelling patterns as a guide to pronunciation.

Exercises

This section has a variety of exercises designed to give you comprehensive practice with the vowel sound as it occurs in words, common phrases, and sentences.

Self-Tests

This section contains mini-tests to help you evaluate your progress. Your ability to recognize and pronounce the sound in words, sentences, and conversational activities will be tested.

For an Encore . . . .

This section is designed to give you practice in using the target vowel in daily life. A variety of listening, reading, and conversational activities are provided at the end of each chapter.

Additional chapters include explanations and exercises for the use of English stress, rhythm, and intonation patterns. Answers to all self-test items are given in Appendix II.

The audio tapes that accompany the manual contain recorded sections of each chapter (a picture of a tape cassette next to an exercise tells you that the exercise is included on the tape). The tapes are designed to provide you with a model of correct pronunciation for each sound covered. Please refer to page vii for a complete outline of the material included on the cassette tapes.

USING THE *ENGLISH PRONUNCIATION FOR SPANISH SPEAKERS* PROGRAM

Now you are ready to begin the program. The only other materials you will need are a cassette recorder to play the tapes and a mirror to help you correctly place your articulators to make the right sound. Find yourself a quiet, comfortable area to practice in; bring along your enthusiasm and determination to improve your speech—*and you're all ready to go!!!*

Before beginning the program, read the first chapter in the manual and play Tape I (Side A) completely to become familiar with the format of the lessons. (Be sure you understand the written explanations in the manual before beginning oral practice.)

Exercises

Rewind the tape to the beginning and look at Exercise A, page 12. Practice the exercise using the directions provided. Repeat the words after the instructor during the pauses. You can stop the tape whenever you like and repeat a section. If you have difficulty at any time, stop the tape and reread the directions for pronouncing the vowel. Check in the mirror to be sure your articulators are in the correct position. Continue with each exercise until you feel you can say the words and sentences easily. Before starting the next section, you should be able to repeat the material after the instructor on the tape without looking at the book.

Self-Tests

After you are happy with your ability to do the exercises, begin the self-tests. The instructions for each self-test are different; read all the directions carefully before beginning. When you finish each test, turn off the recorder and check your answers in Appendix II. If you have any difficulty with the tests, return to the beginning of the chapter and repeat the exercises. The dialogues and paragraphs are the most difficult activities in each chapter; review them often as you progress through the manual.

For an Encore . . . .

When you're content with your pronunciation of the target vowel in the exercises and self-tests, you are ready to progress from the book to "real life" situations. "For an Encore" provides a few suggestions to guide you in making your correct pronunciation of the sound automatic. Try to find other ways to incorporate the sound into your daily routine.

Review Chapters

Review chapters are designed to give you additional practice. Complete the self-tests as you did in the previous chapters. If you have difficulty with one of the vowels, return to the appropriate chapter and review.

Practice Sessions

It is very important to practice as much as possible. Try to follow a definite time schedule. Daily practice sessions are ideal, but if your time is limited, try to practice at least three or four times a week (even if only for 20 to 30 minutes). *We know that reading the book and listening to the tapes is VERY hard work.* **TAKE A BREAK WHEN YOU GET TIRED.** Continue your study session when you feel refreshed. DON'T TRY TO DO IT ALL AT ONCE! **Improvement takes time. BUT, little by little, *you will succeed!***

Keep your tape recorder and cassettes handy to use in the kitchen while you are preparing dinner or in the car while you're driving to work. Practice when you're relaxed, rested, and motivated so you will do your very best. ***PRACTICE MAKES PERFECT!!!***

OTHER WAYS TO IMPROVE YOUR SPEECH

LISTENING to correct pronunciation patterns is as important as practicing them. Take advantage of as many opportunities as possible to hear English being spoken correctly. You can do this by following these suggestions:

1. Watch the evening news on TV. Pay careful attention to the newscaster's pronunciation of words. Repeat some of these words and phrases out loud. *(Your family won't think you are talking to yourself — they'll admire you for trying to improve!)*

2. Listen to radio news stations for 5 or 10 minutes at a time. Repeat common words and phrases after the announcer. *(If anyone gives you a strange look, just tell the person you are practicing your speech!)*

3. When one of your favorite TV shows is on, try to understand the dialogue without watching. *OR*, if you must keep your eyes glued to the screen every minute, wait for the commercials to practice your listening skills without watching.

4. Converse frequently with native American English speakers.

5. Ask your listener if you are pronouncing a specific word correctly. *He or she will be glad to help!*

6. **Most important of all—BE BRAVE!** The exercises are full of common expressions. Use some of them in real conversations. For example, *See you this evening* or *Pleased to meet you* are common phrases you can easily practice. No one will realize that you are doing your homework!!!

Although this program emphasizes pronunciation, the material used in the manual can help you increase your vocabulary also. When you don't understand a word or idiom, look it up in the dictionary. Write the definition in your manual so you won't forget it.

You might be wondering how long it will take before you actually see some improvement in your speech. We believe that **English Pronunciation for Spanish Speakers** provides you with everything you need to improve your speech. If you follow the program as it is outlined, you should notice an improvement in just a few weeks. *Remember — THE MORE YOU PRAC-TICE, THE FASTER YOU WILL IMPROVE!*

Motivation really can contribute to changes in speech. Many aspiring actors and actresses have lost heavy accents in order to become movie stars. We can't guarantee you a movie contract, but we know that following this program will help you to be better understood and to communicate better in your everyday lives. **Good luck!**

TURN THE PAGE AND LET'S GET STARTED!!

A KEY TO PRONOUNCING THE VOWELS
OF AMERICAN ENGLISH

You have probably discovered that there is a big difference between the way words are spelled in English and the way they are pronounced. English spelling patterns are inconsistent and are not always a reliable guide to pronunciation. For example, in the following words, the letter "a" is used to represent *five* different sounds.

hate   father   have   any   saw

Pretty confusing, right? That's why we need a set of symbols in which **each** sound is represented by a *different* symbol. In this program, you will learn the International Phonetic Alphabet (IPA), which is used all over the world. It consists of a set of symbols in which **ONE SYMBOL** always represents **ONE SOUND.**

Many dictionaries do not use the IPA. They use a system of symbols known as *diacritical marks* to help you pronounce words. Since you frequently refer to a dictionary when reading and speaking English, we have included the most common dictionary equivalents of the IPA symbols.

DON'T PANIC! It is not necessary to learn all of the symbols at once. Each sound will be introduced and explained **one at a time.** You will learn the symbols easily as you progress through the book. A pronunciation key* to the different vowels and diphthongs of American English with their IPA and dictionary symbols is presented on the next page. Refer to it often for review.

To help you learn the exact pronunciation of the phonetic symbols and key words, the **Key to Pronouncing the Vowels of American English** on the next page has been recorded at the beginning of Tape 1, Side A. You will hear each phonetic symbol introduced and pronounced twice. Each English key word will also be said two times. Listen carefully to this first recording **before** continuing with the program.

---

*The pronunciation taught is that of "general American" speech which is used by most speakers of American English.

A KEY TO PRONOUNCING THE VOWELS OF AMERICAN ENGLISH*

INTERNATIONAL PHONETIC ALPHABET SYMBOL	DICTIONARY SYMBOL	ENGLISH KEY WORDS	SPANISH KEY WORDS
SECTION ONE			
i	ē	me, tea, bee	sí, día, allí
ɪ	i or ĭ	it, pin	
eɪ	ā	ate, game, they	ley, seis, peine
ɛ	e or ĕ	egg, head, pet	el, perro
æ	a or ă	at, fat, happy	
a	ä or ŏ	hot, father	casa, alto, acá
SECTION TWO			
u	o͞o	you, too, rule	luna, tú
ʊ	oo or o͝o	put, cook	
ʌ	u or ŭ	up, but, come	
oʊ	ō	boat, no, oh	habló, dólar
ɔ	ô	all, boss, caught	
SECTION THREE			
ə	ə	soda, upon	
ɜ	ûr	urn, first, serve	
ɚ	ər	father, after	
aʊ	ou	out, cow, house	auto, causa
aɪ	ī	my, pie, I	aire, hay, bailar
ɔɪ	oi	oil, boy, noise	hoy, oiga, sois

*Spanish key words contain vowels which are close approximations of the American English target sound. They are not always technically equal examples.

Definitions

As you progress through this manual, you will frequently see the terms *vowels,* *diphthongs,* and *articulators.* We will now define these terms for you.

VOWEL: A vowel is a speech sound produced with vibrating vocal cords and a continuous unrestricted flow of air coming from the mouth. The most well-known vowels in both English and Spanish are

$$A \qquad E \qquad I \qquad O \qquad and \qquad U.$$

DIPHTHONG: A diphthong is a combination of two vowel sounds. It begins as one vowel and ends as another. During the production of a diphthong, your articulators glide from the position of the first vowel to the position of the second. For example, when pronouncing "ei" as in "peine" or "vein" (vena), your articulators glide from the vowel "e" to the vowel "i." Diphthongs in Spanish include [au], [eɪ], [aɪ], and [ɔɪ] ("au", "ei", "ay", and "oy" or "oi"). In English, the most common diphthongs are [au], [eɪ], [aɪ], [ɔɪ], and [ou].

ARTICULATORS: The articulators are the different parts of the mouth area that we use when speaking, such as the lips, tongue, teeth, and jaw.

The various vowel sounds are affected by the changing shape and position of your articulators. The different vowels are created by:

A. **The position of your tongue in the mouth.** For example, the tongue is high in the mouth for the vowel [i] as in "see" or "sí," but is low in the mouth for the vowel [a] as in "hot" or "casa."

B. **The shape of your lips.** For example, the lips are very rounded for the vowel [u] as in "new" or "luna," but are spread for [i] as in "see" or "sí."

C. **The size of your jaw opening.** For example, the jaw is open much wider for [a] as in "hot" or "casa" than it is for the diphthong [eɪ] as in "pay" or "peine."

PRONOUNCING SECTION I VOWELS

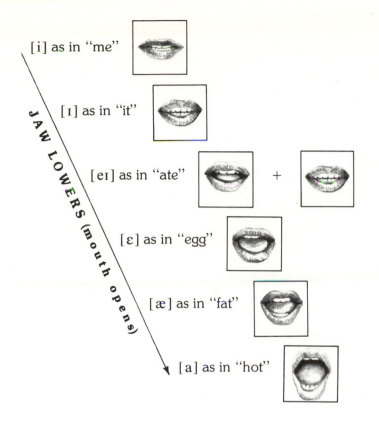

[i] as in "me"

[ɪ] as in "it"

[eɪ] as in "ate"   +

[ε] as in "egg"

[æ] as in "fat"

JAW LOWERS (mouth opens)

[a] as in "hot"

You can see in the pictures how the jaw moves from a closed position to an open one during pronunciation of the vowel sequence [i] [ɪ] [eɪ] [ε] [æ] [a]. Becoming familiar with this progression and understanding the relationship of one vowel to another will help you with your pronunciation of the vowels in Section I of this manual. Examples:

> The phonetic symbol [ɪ] represents a sound between [i] and [eɪ]. It is pronounced with the jaw and tongue raised more than for [eɪ], but not as much as for [i].

> The symbol [æ] represents a sound between [ε] and [a]. [æ] is pronounced with the jaw open more than for [ε], but not as much as for [a].

This may seem a bit confusing at first. Refer to these pictures whenever you have difficulty pronouncing any of the vowels in Section I. Repeat the sequence [i] [ɪ] [eɪ] [ε] [æ] [a] several times. Be sure to **see** and **feel** the progressive dropping of your tongue and jaw as you pronounce each sound.

PRONOUNCING SECTION II VOWELS

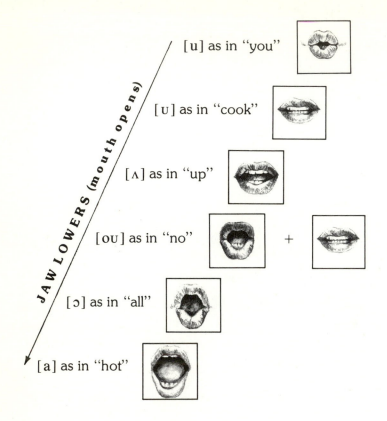

[u] as in "you"

[ʊ] as in "cook"

[ʌ] as in "up"

[oʊ] as in "no"   +

[ɔ] as in "all"

[a] as in "hot"

JAW LOWERS (mouth opens)

Once again you can see how the jaw moves from a closed position to an open one during the pronunciation of a vowel sequence. Practice pronouncing the series several times. Place your hand under your chin and **feel** your jaw drop with the pronunciation of each vowel.

Refer to these pictures whenever you are confused about the pronunciation of any of the vowels in Section II of this book. Repeat the sequence [u] [ʊ] [ʌ] [oʊ] [ɔ] [a] several times. You'll be able to **see** and **feel** your jaw lower as you pronounce the vowels in the series. **TRY IT NOW! IT REALLY WORKS!!!**

```
*****************************************************
```

[i] as in *ME* *TEA* and *BEE*
⟨DICTIONARY MARK: ē⟩

AND

[ɪ] as in *IT* and *PIN*
⟨DICTIONARY MARK: ĭ⟩

```
*****************************************************
```

PRONOUNCING [i]

LIPS:	are tense and in a "smile" position.
JAW:	is completely raised.
TONGUE:	is high near the roof of the mouth.

The sound [i] in English is similar to stressed "í" in Spanish. ([i] is actually longer and more prolonged than Spanish "í".)

SPANISH KEY WORDS WITH [i]

Spanish words with this sound are spelled with "i" or "í".

KEY WORDS: *iba* *vino* *día* *allí*

POSSIBLE PRONUNCIATION PROBLEMS FOR THE SPANISH SPEAKER

Pronunciation problems occur because of confusing English spelling patterns and the similarity of [i] and [ɪ] (the sound to be described next). It's easy to understand why some Spanish speakers are afraid to say words like *"sheet"* or *"beach."*

EXAMPLES: When you substitute [ɪ] for [i]:   *sheep* becomes *ship*
                                              eat becomes *it*

DON'T WORRY! You already know the [i] *sound in Spanish. Remember to feel tension in your lips, tongue, and jaw.* [i] *is a LONG sound; be sure to prolong it. SMILE when you say* [i]; *WE GUARANTEE it's EASY to say* [i]*!!!*

The following words should all be pronounced with [i]. Repeat them carefully after your teacher or the instructor on the tape.

[i] **At the Beginning**	[i] **In the Middle**	[i] **At the End**
eat	mean	he
eel	need	bee
east	keen	key
easy	deep	tea
each	seal	fee
even	leave	tree
equal	reach	knee
eagle	scene	free
eager	please	she
either	police	agree

[i] **spelled:**

"e"	"ee"	"ea"	"ie" or "ei"
he	see	east	niece
we	eel	lean	brief
me	deed	team	piece
scene	heel	cheap	belief
these	needy	peach	either

Less frequent spelling patterns for [i] consist of the letters "i" and "eo".

EXAMPLES: police   people

> **_HINTS:_**   a.   The letters "ee" are usually pronounced [i].
>
> EXAMPLES: **s**ee   gr**ee**n   f**ee**t   fr**ee**dom
>
> b.   The letters "ei" and "ie" are usually pronounced [i].
>
> EXAMPLES: **ei**ther   rec**ei**ve   p**ie**ce   gr**ie**f

Note: The picture of a tape cassette next to an exercise tells you that this exercise is included on the tape.

EXERCISE B

Read the following pairs of [i] words aloud. *PROLONG* the [i] vowel before the consonant. (The dots are there to remind you to lengthen the [i].) **This exercise is not on the tape.**

1. fee   fee . . . . . . .d   (feed)
2. see   see . . . . . . .d   (seed)
3. pea   pea . . . . . . .s   (peas)
4. bee   bee . . . . . . .s   (bees)
5. tea   tea . . . . . .m   (team)

 ## EXERCISE C

The boldface words in the following phrases and sentences should all be pronounced with the vowel [i]. Repeat them carefully after your teacher or the instructor on the tape.

1. **See** you next **week**.
2. **See** you this **evening**.
3. **See** you at **three**.
4. **See** what I **mean**?
5. **Pleased** to **meet** you.
6. **Steve eats cream cheese**.
7. **Lee** has a **reason** for **leaving**.
8. **She received** her **teaching degree**.
9. A friend in **need**, is a friend **indeed**!
10. They **reached** a **peace agreement**.
11. The **dean** will **be free** at **three**.
12. **We** will **keep** the **secret**.
13. Spring is the **peak season** for **peaches**.
14. Did you **see Pete** at the **meeting**?
15. I **feel** a **breeze** through the **trees**.

Repeat each of the following words after your teacher or the instructor on the tape. Circle only the words that are pronounced with [i].

1. (steam)
2. stem
3. easy
4. window
5. Easter
6. Christmas
7. holiday
8. difficult
9. three
10. six
11. pencil
12. season
13. winter
14. spring
15. even
16. agree
17. been
18. bean
19. ice
20. meat

SELF-TEST II (Correct answers may be found in Appendix II on page 162.)

Read each series of four words out loud. Circle the **ONE** word in each group of four that is **NOT** pronounced with [i] **This self-test is not on the tape.**

EXAMPLE:	keep	lean	(fit)	piece
1.	bead	great	leave	tea
2.	eight	either	believe	niece
3.	scene	women	these	even
4.	need	been	sleep	thirteen
5.	police	thief	machine	vision
6.	pretty	wheat	sweet	cream
7.	people	bread	deal	east
8.	tin	teen	steam	receive
9.	leave	live	leaf	lease
10.	steep	Steve	easy	still

PRONOUNCING [ɪ]

LIPS:	**are relaxed and slightly parted.**
JAW:	**is slightly lower than for** [i].
TONGUE:	**is high, but lower than for** [i].

POSSIBLE PRONUNCIATION PROBLEMS FOR THE SPANISH SPEAKER

The vowel [ɪ] does not exist in Spanish and may be difficult for you to recognize and say. You probably substitute the more familiar [i] sound.

EXAMPLES: When you substitute [i] for [ɪ]: ***hit*** becomes ***heat***
itch becomes ***each***

As you practice the exercises, remember NOT to "smile" and tense your lips as you would for [i]. [ɪ] **is a SHORT, QUICK sound; your lips should barely move as you say it.**

 # EXERCISE A

lado A
14.16

The following words should all be pronounced with [ɪ]. Repeat them carefully after your teacher or the instructor on the tape.*

[ɪ] **At the Beginning**	[ɪ] **In the Middle**
is	pin
if	lift
it	give
ill	miss
itch	simple
into	winter
ink	listen
inch	timid
issue	minute
instant	little

*The vowel [ɪ] does not occur at the end of words in English.

[ɪ] **spelled:**

"y"	"ui"	"i"
gym	build	sin
syrup	quick	lips
symbol	quilt	with
system	guilty	gift
rhythm	guitar	differ

Less frequent spelling patterns for [ɪ] consist of the letters "o", "e", "u", and "ee".

EXAMPLES: w**o**men pr**e**tty b**u**sy b**ee**n

> **HINT:** The most common spelling pattern for [ɪ] is the letter "i" followed by a final consonant.
>
> EXAMPLES: w**in** th**is** h**it** tr**ip** beg**in**

EXERCISE B

The boldface words in the following phrases and sentences should all be pronounced with the [ɪ] vowel. Repeat them carefully after your teacher or the instructor on the tape.

1. **This is it**.
2. What **is this**?
3. **This is** my **sister**.
4. **This is Miss Smith**.
5. **This is big business**.
6. **Bill is still ill**.
7. **This winter** was **bitter**.
8. **Give** the **list** to **Lynn**.
9. My **little sister is timid**.
10. The **picture is** a **big hit**.
11. **Is** the **building finished**?
12. **Bring this gift** to **Jim**.
13. I **will sit in** a **minute**.
14. **Which quilt did** you **pick**?
15. **Did** you **give him his gift**?

SELF-TEST I   (Correct answers may be found in Appendix II on page 162.)

Read each series of four words out loud. Circle the **ONE** word in each group
of four that is **NOT** pronounced with [ɪ]. **This self-test is not on the tape.**

EXAMPLE: rhythm   build   (seize)   finish

1. fifty   sixty   eighteen   six
2. window   sill   widow   wipe
3. freedom   sympathy   simple   symbol
4. building   smile   little   guitar
5. pistol   resign   fiddle   whistle
6. quit   criminal   crime   brittle
7. sheep   flip   tickle   fifteen
8. pretty   been   feet   fit
9. business   women   leave   lift
10. piece   pity   typical   tips

 ## SELF-TEST II   (Correct answers may be found in Appendix II on page 163.)

Listen carefully to your teacher or the tape as the following pairs of words are
presented. **ONE** word in each pair is pronounced with [ɪ]. Circle the number
of the word with the vowel [ɪ].

EXAMPLE: The instructor says: **mitt**   **meat**
                        You circle: ①   2

1. ① 2   6. 1 ②
2. 1 ②   7. 1 ②
3. ① 2   8. ① 2
4. 1 ②   9. 1 ②
5. ① 2   10. ① 2

```
************************************
```
REVIEW OF [i] AND [ɪ]
```
************************************
```

🎙 ORAL EXERCISE

Repeat the pairs of words and sentences carefully after your teacher or the instructor on the tape. REMEMBER to **SMILE** and feel the tension in your lips when you repeat the words with [i] and to **RELAX** your muscles as you pronounce the [ɪ] words.

	[i]	[ɪ]
1.	least	list
2.	seat	sit
3.	heat	hit
4.	feet	fit
5.	leave	live
6.	Heat it now.	Hit it now.
7.	Change the wheel.	Change the will.
8.	Did you feel it?	Did you fill it?
9.	The meal was big.	The mill was big.
10.	He will leave.	He will live.

11. Please **sit** in the **seat**.
        [ɪ]   [i]
12. He **did** a good **deed**.
        [ɪ]   [i]
13. **Phil** doesn't **feel** well.
      [ɪ]   [i]
14. **Lynn** ate **lean** meat.
      [ɪ]   [i]
15. Potato **chips** are **cheap**.
        [ɪ]   [i]

SELF-TEST I (Correct answers may be found in Appendix II on page 163.)

Your teacher or the instructor on the tape will say only **ONE** word in each of the following pairs. Listen carefully and circle the word that you hear.

EXAMPLES: a. (meat)   mit
            b. feel   (fill)

✓1. field   (filled)   ✓6. team   Tim
- 2. bean   (bin)   ✓7. sleep   slip
✓3. neat   (knit)   ✓8. green   (grin)
✓4. deal   (dill)   ✓9. heel   (hill)
✓5. beat   (bit)   ✓10. week   wick

SELF-TEST II (Correct answers may be found in Appendix II on page 163.)

Your teacher or the instructor on the tape will present the following sentences using **ONLY ONE** of the choices. Listen carefully and circle the word (and vowel) used.

EXAMPLE:	You need a new	(wheel	(will).
		[i]	[ɪ]
✓1.	They cleaned the	(sheep	ship).
		[i]	[ɪ]
✓2.	Will he	(leave	live)?
		[i]	[ɪ]
✓3.	The boy was	(beaten	bitten).
		[i]	[ɪ]
✓4.	His clothes are	(neat	knit).
		[i]	[ɪ]
✓5.	She has plump	(cheeks)	chicks).
		[i]	[ɪ]
— 6.	I like low	(heels	hills).
		[i]	[ɪ]
— 7.	The children will	(sleep	slip).
		[i]	[ɪ]
✓8.	I heard every	(beat	bit).
		[i]	[ɪ]

9.   They stored the   (beans   bins).
                                   [i]   [ɪ]
10.   Everyone talks about the   (heat   hit).
                                   [i]   [ɪ]

....

After checking your answers in Appendix II, read each of the sentences twice. Use the first word in the first reading and the contrast word in the second reading.

SELF-TEST III   (Correct answers may be found in Appendix II on page 164.)

Read each of the following sentences aloud. In the brackets above each italicized word, write the phonetic symbol ([i] or [ɪ]) representing the vowel in that word. **This self-test is not on the tape.**

             [i]   [ɪ]   [i]
EXAMPLE: The *field* was *filled with* flowers.
             [ ][ ]   [ ]
1.   Take a *dip in* the *deep* water.
             [ ] [ ]   [ ]
2.   They *picked Tim* for the *team*.
             [ ] [ ]   [ ] [ ]
3.   *Please beat* the *sweet cream*.
         [ ][ ][ ][ ]   [ ]
4.   *She will sit in* the *seat*.
             [ ]   [ ]   [ ]
5.   The *heat* wave *hit* the *city*.
             [ ]   [ ]   [ ]
6.   *Jean* has *been* cooking *beans*.
                 [ ] [ ][ ]
7.   His pet *eel* is *still ill*!
             [ ]   [ ][ ] [ ]
8.   At *least* my *list is finished*.
         [ ][ ] [ ]   [ ]
9.   *Is he* at *ease* on *skis*?
             [ ]   [ ]   [ ] [ ]
10. *These slippers* don't *fit* my *feet*.

20   REVIEW OF [i] AND [ɪ]

SELF-TEST IV   (Correct answers may be found in Appendix II on page 164.)

Listen carefully to your teacher or the tape as the following dialogue is presented. CIRCLE all the words pronounced with [i], and UNDERLINE all the words with [ɪ].

. . . .

JIM: Hi, Tina! Do you have a **minute**?

TINA: Yes, Jim. What is it?

JIM: My sister is in the city on business. We will eat dinner out tonight. Can you recommend a place to eat?

TINA: There is a fine seafood restaurant on Fifth Street. The fish is fresh and the shrimp is great. But it isn't cheap!

JIM: That's OK. It will be "feast today, famine tomorrow!" I'll have to eat "frijoles" the rest of the week!

. . . .

After checking your answers in the Appendix, practice the dialogue out loud with a friend. Remember to **smile** and **tense** your lips for [i] and to **relax** them when pronouncing [ɪ] words.

FOR AN ENCORE . . . .

Conversation

Plan at least three occasions when you have to use phrases of introduction. Use the following key phrases:

"This is (my sister Jill) _____ " (name of person).
"Pleased to meet you, (Mr./Mrs./Miss Smith) _____ " (name).
"I'd like you to meet (my friend Tim, my sister, etc.) _____ ."

You can also use the phrase *"This is _____ "* when identifying yourself on the phone. *("This is Miss Gomez.")*

REMEMBER TO KEEP PRACTICING!!!

⟨⟨⟨ *WE GUARANTEE IT'S EASY TO SAY* [ɪ] *AND* [i] ⟩⟩⟩

```
*****************************************************
```

[eɪ] as in *ATE   GAME*   and   *THEY*
⟨DICTIONARY MARK: ā⟩

```
*****************************************************
```

PRONOUNCING [eɪ]

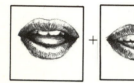 +

LIPS: are spread and unround.

JAW: rises with the tongue and closes slightly.

TONGUE: glides from midlevel to near the roof of the mouth.

[eɪ] is a diphthong. It begins with [e] and ends with [ɪ]. [eɪ] is pronounced the same way as the Spanish letters "ei" or "ey".

SPANISH KEY WORDS WITH [eɪ]

Spanish words with this sound are spelled with "ey" or "ei".

KEY WORDS: *ley*   *reyes*   *veinte*   *peine*   *reina*

POSSIBLE PRONUNCIATION PROBLEMS
FOR THE SPANISH SPEAKER

Pronunciation problems occur because of confusing English spelling patterns and the similarity of [eɪ] and [ɛ] (the sound to be described in the next chapter).

EXAMPLE: When you substitute [ɛ] for [eɪ]:   *late*   becomes *let*
paper becomes *pepper*

RELAX! You already use the diphthong [eɪ] in Spanish. [eɪ] is a LONG sound; be sure to raise your jaw and prolong it or you will substitute the shorter, quicker [ɛ] vowel (as in "perro"). Think of the Spanish key words "ley", "rey", and "veinte" as you practice the exercises and *you'll SAY* [eɪ] *the right WAY!!!*

EXERCISE A

The following words should all be pronounced with [eɪ]. Repeat them carefully after your teacher or the instructor on the tape.

[eɪ] **At the Beginning**	[eɪ] **In the Middle**	[eɪ] **At the End**
ate	same	way
ape	rain	say
age	came	day
aim	lake	lay
ale	date	May
able	table	they
ache	place	obey
eight	break	away
April	paint	stay
apron	paper	weigh

[eɪ] **spelled:**

"a"	"ai"	"ay"	"eigh"
late	main	day	eight
sane	fail	bay	weigh
safe	wait	hay	sleigh
hate	grain	ray	freight
lady	raise	play	neighbor

Less frequent spelling patterns for [eɪ] consist of the letters "ea", "ey", and "ei".

EXAMPLES: br**ea**k gr**ea**t th**ey** gr**ey** v**ei**n

EXERCISE B

The boldface words in the following phrases and sentences should all be pronounced with the diphthong [eɪ]. Repeat them carefully after your teacher or the instructor on the tape.

1. **Wake** up!
2. **gain weight**
3. What's your **name**?
4. **late date**
5. **Take** it **away**!
6. **Make haste** not **waste**!

7. **April** showers
   April showers bring **May** flowers.
8. **they played**
   They played a **great game**.
9. on his **paper**
   Blake got an **"A"** on his **paper**.
10. **lady's age**
    The **lady's age** is **eighty-eight**.
11. **raisin cake**
    It's a **shame** to **waste** the **raisin cake**.
12. **came late**
    The **plane** from **Spain came late**.
13. **away** on **vacation**
    The **neighbors** are **away** on **vacation**.

24   [eɪ] as in ATE

14. **train station**
    Ray will **wait** at the **train station**.
15. **today's paper**
    They made a **mistake** in **today's paper**.

SELF-TEST I (Correct answers may be found in Appendix II on page 165.)

Read the following **"shopping list"** out loud. (You are going to buy the items with the [eɪ] sound.) Circle **ONLY** the items pronounced with [eɪ]. **This self-test is not on the tape.**

(steak)	lettuce	mayonnaise	cereal
bread	raisins	melon	bananas
cake	tomatoes	bacon	baking soda
potatoes	crackers	peas	ice cream
grapes	celery	gravy	carrots
toothpaste	peas	squash	paper plates

 ## SELF-TEST II (Correct answers may be found in Appendix II on page 165.)

Listen carefully to your teacher or the tape as ten three-word series are presented. **ONE** word in each group will be pronounced with [eɪ]. Circle the number of the word with the diphthong [eɪ].

EXAMPLE: The instructor says: hat   hot   hate
                        You circle: 1   2   ③

✓1. ①   2   3   ✓6. ①   2   3
2. 1   2   3   ✓7. 1   ②   3
✓3. 1   2   ③   ✓8. ①   2   3
✓4. 1   ②   3   ✓9. 1   ②   3
✓5. ①   2   3   ✓10. ①   2   3

SELF-TEST III

(Correct answers may be found in Appendix II on page 165.)

Read each four-word series out loud. Circle the **ONE** word in each group of four that is **NOT** pronounced with [eɪ]. **This self-test is not on the tape.**

EXAMPLE: April   May   vacation   (sad)

1.	practice	plate	play	place
2.	stay	aid	plaid	raid
3.	neighbor	freight	height	eighty
4.	head	great	break	came
5.	shave	any	staple	pays
6.	America	Asia	Spain	Maine
7.	laid	crayon	seven	tame
8.	great	grace	grey	greedy
9.	obtain	awake	create	breakfast
10.	snake	obey	breath	complain

SELF-TEST IV

(Correct answers may be found in Appendix II on page 165.)

Listen carefully to your teacher or the tape as the following paragraph is read. Circle all words pronounced with [eɪ].

· ·

(Babe) Ruth was a (famous) baseball player. He was born and raised in an orphanage in Baltimore. He first played for the Boston Red Sox but was later traded to the New York Yankees. He made 714 home runs and became a baseball legend. He was named to the Baseball Hall of Fame. The last team he played for was the Boston Braves. He died in 1948. Many say he was the greatest player of his day.

· ·

After checking your answers in Appendix II, read the paragraph aloud. Concentrate on the correct pronunciation of the [eɪ] words.

FOR AN ENCORE ....

Reading

Turn to the sports section of your newspaper. Read about any game that was recently played. Underline all words pronounced with [eɪ]. Tape yourself reading the article aloud or read it to a friend. Practice the [eɪ] words several times.

PRACTICE MAKES PERFECT!!!

⟨⟨⟨ *S<u>AY</u>* [<u>eɪ</u>] *the RIGHT W<u>AY</u>* ⟩⟩⟩

side

****

[ɛ] as in *EGG PET* and *HEAD*

⟨**DICTIONARY MARK:** ĕ⟩

****

PRONOUNCING [ɛ]

LIPS:	are slightly spread and unround.
JAW:	is open more than for [eɪ].
TONGUE:	is midlevel in the mouth.

The vowel [ɛ] in English is similar to the sound of the letter "e" in certain Spanish words. ([ɛ] is actually shorter and quicker than Spanish "e".)

SPANISH KEY WORDS WITH [ɛ]

Spanish words have this sound when "e" comes before consonants other than "s" or "z".

 KEY WORDS: *el   entra   usted   perro*

POSSIBLE PRONUNCIATION PROBLEMS FOR THE SPANISH SPEAKER

Pronunciation problems occur because of confusing English spelling patterns and the similarity between [ɛ] and other sounds.

EXAMPLES: If you replace [ɛ] with [eɪ]: **pen** sounds like **pain**
  If you replace [ɛ] with [æ]: **met** sounds like **mat**

When pronouncing [ɛ], open your mouth **wider** than for [eɪ] but less than for [æ] (the sound to be discussed in the next chapter). Think of the Spanish key words **el** and **perro** and you'll **NEVER make an ERROR on [ɛ]!**

EXERCISE A

The following words should all be pronounced with [ɛ]. Repeat them carefully after your teacher or the instructor on the tape.*

[ɛ] **At the Beginning**	[ɛ] **In the Middle**
any	bed
end	next
egg	west
edge	rest
else	bent
every	many
effort	bread
error	fence
elephant	present

[ɛ] spelled:

"e"	**"ea"**
yes	head
red	lead
sell	dead
seven	meadow
never	measure

Less frequent spelling patterns for [ɛ] consist of the letters "a", "ai", "ie", "ue", and "eo".

EXAMPLES: **a**ny ag**ai**n fr**ie**nd g**ue**st l**eo**pard

HINTS: a. The most common spelling pattern for [ɛ] is the letter "e" before a consonant in a stressed syllable.

EXAMPLES: l**e**t am**e**nd att**e**ntive pl**e**nty

b. The letter "e" before "l" is usually pronounced [ɛ].

EXAMPLES: w**el**l t**el**ephone f**el**t s**el**dom

c. The letters "ea" before "d" are usually pronounced [ɛ].

EXAMPLES: thr**ead** ah**ead** r**ead**y d**ead**

*The vowel [ɛ] does not occur at the end of words in English.

EXERCISE B

Repeat the following pairs of words after your teacher or the instructor on the tape. When pronouncing the words with [ɛ], be sure to lower your jaw a bit **more** than for [eɪ].

[ɛ]	[eɪ]
met	mate
bet	bait
fed	fade
less	lace
pen	pain
let	late
wet	weight
get	gate
red	raid
wed	wade

 EXERCISE C

The boldface words in the following phrases and sentences should all be pronounced with the vowel [ɛ]. Repeat them carefully after your teacher or the instructor on the tape.

1. You **said** it!
2. **head** of **lettuce**
3. **best friend**

4. **healthy** and **wealthy**
5. **bent fender**
6. **never better**

7. at **ten**
   Breakfast is **ready** at **ten**.
8. **left** a **message**
   Fred left a **message**.
9. **let** me **get**
   Let me **get** some **rest**!
10. don't **forget**
    Don't **forget** to **send** the **letter**.
11. in **September**
    The **weather** is **better** in **September**.

12. **went** to **bed.**
    Wendy went to **bed** at **seven**.
13. **extra pencils**
    Are there **any extra pencils**?
14. **leather belts**
    Leather belts are **very expensive.**
15. **help yourself**
    Help yourself to **bread** and **jelly**.

SELF-TEST I   (Correct answers may be found in Appendix II on page 166.)

Repeat the following words after your teacher or the instructor on the tape.
Circle the letter "e" in each word that is pronounced [ɛ]. **(Only ONE "e" in
each word is actually pronounced [ɛ].)**

EXAMPLES: a. t(e)l e v i s i o n
            b. d e v(e)l o p

1. D e c e m b e r
2. r e j e c t
3. e v e r y
4. e l e v a t o r
5. s e v e n t e e n

6. e l e v e n
7. r e m e m b e r
8. r e f e r e n c e
9. s e c r e t a r y
10. t e l e p h o n e

SELF-TEST II   (Correct answers may be found in Appendix II on page 166.)

Read each series of four words out loud. Circle the **ONE** word in each group
of four that is **NOT** pronounced with [ɛ]. **This exerise is not on the tape.**

EXAMPLE: Mexico   America   (Egypt)   Texas

1. any   crazy   anywhere   many
2. paper   letter   send   pencil
3. seven   eleven   eight   twenty
4. health   wreath   breath   wealth
5. reading   ready   already   head
6. present   precious   preview   president

[ɛ] as in EGG   **31**

7.	November	February	September	April
8.	guess	guest	cues	question
9.	thread	threat	fresh	theater
10.	mean	meant	meadow	met

SELF-TEST III   (Correct answers may be found in Appendix II on page 166.)

Listen carefully as your teacher or the instructor on the tape presents ten sentences. Some words that should be pronounced with [ɛ] will be said INCORRECTLY. Circle **"C"** for **Correct** or **"I"** for **Incorrect** to indicate whether the [ɛ] word in each sentence is pronounced properly.

Sentence #	Response		
EXAMPLE a:	Ⓒ	I	(Who **fed** the fish?)
EXAMPLE b:	C	Ⓘ	(I got **wait** in the rain.)
1.	C	I
2.	C	I
3.	C	I
4.	C	I
5.	C	I
6.	C	I
7.	C	I
8.	C	I
9.	C	I
10.	C	I

SELF-TEST IV   (Correct answers may be found in Appendix II on page 167.)

Read the following dialogue aloud. Circle all words that should be pronounced with the vowel [ɛ]. **This self-test is not on the tape.**

· ·

MS. NELSON: "(Nelson) (Temporary) (Help.)" Ms. Nelson speaking. Can I
                help you?

MR. PEREZ: Yes, this is Pepe Perez. I need a temporary secretary.

MS. NELSON: What kind of secretary do you need?

MR. PEREZ: The BEST! That means well educated and with excellent
                clerical skills.

MS. NELSON: Anything else?

MR. PEREZ: Yes. I like pretty secretaries with good legs. Get what I mean?

MS. NELSON: Yes, I do. I have the best secretary for you. I'll send one
                Wednesday at ten.

MR. PEREZ: Thanks. It's been a pleasure talking to you.

MS. NELSON: Evelyn, get me Ted Benson's file. He's an excellent secretary
                and has very good legs!!!

· ·

After checking your answers in Appendix II, practice the dialogue out loud again. This time, try it with a friend! Carefully pronounce all [ɛ] words.

FOR AN ENCORE ·

Listening

Listen to the weather report on radio or TV. Make a list of all the words you hear pronounced with [ɛ]. After the broadcast, practice them aloud (*i.e.: temperature, weather, wet, seventy degrees*, etc.).

PRACTICE YOUR [ɛ] **AGAIN and AGAIN and** ·

⟨⟨⟨ *YOU'LL NEVER MAKE AN ERROR ON* [ɛ] ⟩⟩⟩

```
************************************************
```

[æ] as in *AT* *FAT* and *HAPPY*

⟨DICTIONARY MARK: a or ă⟩

```
************************************************
```

PRONOUNCING [æ]

LIPS:	are spread.
JAW:	is open wider than for [ɛ].
TONGUE:	is low near the floor of the mouth.

POSSIBLE PRONUNCIATION PROBLEMS
FOR THE SPANISH SPEAKER

The vowel [æ] does not exist in Spanish and may be difficult for you to hear and produce. Also, you might always pronounce the letter "a" the Spanish way!

EXAMPLES: If you say [a] instead of [æ], **hat** will sound like **hot**
If you say [ɛ] instead of [æ], **bad** will sound like **bed**

When producing the vowel [æ], remember to spread your lips and open your mouth. **But**—don't open it too wide or you will find yourself substituting [a] (the vowel to be studied in the next chapter) instead! *PRACTICE, PRAC-TICE, PRACTICE AND you'll HAVE [æ] down PAT!!!*

EXERCISE A

The following words should all be pronounced with the [æ] sound. Repeat them as accurately as possible after your teacher or the instructor on the tape.*

[æ] At the Beginning

at
am
and
ask
apple
after
actor
angry
absent
animal

[æ] In the Middle

cat
map
have
back
last
black
flag
happy
class
rapid

A less frequent spelling pattern for [æ] consists of the letters "au."

EXAMPLES: la**u**gh   la**u**ghter

EXERCISE B

Repeat the following pairs of words after your teacher or the instructor on the tape. When repeating the [æ] words, be sure to open your mouth **more** than for [ɛ].

[æ]

had
mat
pat
land
past
tan
sad
and
lad
add

[ɛ]

head
met
pet
lend
pest
ten
said
end
led
Ed

*The vowel [æ] does not occur at the end of words in English.

 **EXERCISE C**

The boldface words in the following phrases and sentences should all be pronounced with the vowel [æ]. Repeat them carefully after your teacher or the instructor on the tape.

1. **last chance**
2. I'll be **back.**
3. **at** a **glance**

4. **wrap** it up
5. Is **that** a **fact?**
6. **clap** your **hands**

7. **pack** of **matches**
   Hand me a **pack** of **matches.**
8. to **catch**
   I **have** to **catch** a **cab.**
9. **can't stand**
   Ralph can't stand carrots.
10. **black jack**
    The **gambler** plays **black jack.**
11. **happily married**
    He's a **happily married man.**
12. **ham sandwich**
    Pam had a **ham sandwich.**
13. **hat** and **jacket**
    Pack my **hat** and **jacket.**
14. **math exam**
    He **passed** the **math exam.**
15. **last laugh**
    He who **laughs last, laughs** best!

Listen carefully to your teacher or the tape as each three-word series is presented. Only **ONE** word in each series will have the [æ] vowel. Circle the number of the word with the [æ] sound.

EXAMPLE: Your teacher says: **knack** **knock** **neck**
You circle: ① 2 3

1. ① 2 3
2. 1 2 ③
3. ① 2 3
4. 1 ② 3
5. 1 2 ③

6. ① 2 3
7. 1 2 ③
8. 1 ② 3
9. ① 2 3
10. 1 ② 3

SELF-TEST II (Correct answers may be found in Appendix II on page 167.)

Read the following letter aloud. Circle all words that should be pronounced with the vowel [æ]. **This self-test is not on the tape.**

· ·

Dear Mom and Dad,
 At last we are in San Francisco. It's a fabulous city! As we stand at the top of Telegraph Hill we can see Alcatraz. We plan to catch a cable car and visit Grant Avenue in Chinatown. After that, we'll have tea in the Japanese Gardens. Yesterday we drank wine in Napa Valley. We also passed through the National Park. Our last stop is Disneyland in Los Angeles. We'll be back next Saturday.

Love,

Gladys

P.S. We need cash. Please send money fast!

· ·

After checking your answers in Appendix II, practice reading the letter again. Concentrate on the correct pronunciation of the [æ] words.

Repeat the following words after your teacher or the instructor on the tape. Circle the **letter "a"** in each word that is pronounced [æ].

(Only ONE "a" in each word is actually pronounced [æ].**)**

EXAMPLES: a. b a n (a) n a
　　　　　　 b. (a) n i m a l

1. p(a)r a d i s e
2. (A)f r i c a
3. C(a)l i f o r n i a
4. f(a)s c i n a t e
5. A l(a)s k a

6. a t t(a)c k
7. S(a)t u r d a y
8. C(a)n a d a
9. D(a)l l a s
10. p(a)c k a g e

FOR AN ENCORE ....

Reading

Select a set of directions for something (i.e.: using an appliance, assembling an item, etc.). Circle all words pronounced with [æ]. Read the directions aloud step by step to another person. Ask the person to repeat the directions back to you. Practice the words your listener has difficulty understanding.

PRACTICE * PRACTICE *** PRACTICE**

⟨⟨⟨ *YOU'LL H_AVE* [æ] *DOWN P_AT* ⟩⟩⟩

```
*********************************************
```

[a] as in *ARM   HOT*   and   *FATHER*

⟨DICTIONARY MARK: ä⟩

```
*********************************************
```

PRONOUNCING [a]

LIPS:	are completely apart in a *"yawning"* position.
JAW:	is lower than for any other vowel.
TONGUE:	is flat on the floor of the mouth.

The sound [a] in English is the same as stressed "á" in Spanish.

SPANISH KEY WORDS WITH [a]

Spanish words with this sound are spelled with "a" or "á".

KEY WORDS: *casa   palabra   dará   acá*

POSSIBLE PRONUNCIATION PROBLEMS
FOR THE SPANISH SPEAKER

Irregular English spelling patterns are the main reason you have pronunciation problems with the vowel [a]. The letter "o" in English is frequently pronounced [a], like the "a" in *casa* or *acá.*

EXAMPLES: If you substitute [oʊ] for [a]:   ***not*** will sound like ***note***
If you substitute [ʌ]   for [a]:   ***not*** will sound like ***nut***
If you substitute [ɔ]   for [a]:   ***cot*** will sound like ***caught***

Very confusing, right? But stop worrying!! You already pronounce [a] in Spanish. When practicing the following exercises, ***think of the Spanish key words "CASA" and "ACÁ"; we're POSITIVE you'll be ON TARGET with [a]!!!***

EXERCISE A

The following words should all be pronounced with [a]. Repeat them accurately after your teacher or the instructor on the tape.*

[a] **At the Beginning**	[a] **In the Middle**
on	top
odd	cot
arm	lock
are	shop
arch	wasp
oxen	watch
honest	block
option	March
artist	rocket
	problem

[a] **spelled:**

"a"	**"o"**
want	fox
wallet	hot
dark	spot
father	opera
pardon	follow

> **HINTS:**
> a. The letter "o" followed by "b", "d", "g", "p", "t" or "ck" is usually pronounced [a].
>
> EXAMPLES: **rob**in **rod** **log** s**top** **lot** **pock**et
>
> b. The letter "a" followed by "r" is usually pronounced [a].
>
> EXAMPLES: **far**m al**arm** c**ar**t st**ar**t **ar**e

*The vowel [a] does not occur at the end of words in English.

EXERCISE B

Repeat the following pairs of words after your teacher or the instructor on the tape. Be sure to open your mouth wider when pronouncing the words with the [a] vowel.

[a]	[æ]
cop	cap
hot	hat
pot	pat
odd	add
mop	map
top	tap
log	lag
lock	lack
cob	cab
solid	salad

EXERCISE C

The boldface words in the following phrases and sentences should all be pronounced with the vowel [a]. Repeat them as accurately as possible after your teacher or the instructor on the tape.

1. **alarm clock**
2. **stock market**
3. **not far apart**
4. **top** to **bottom**
5. **cops** and **robbers**
6. **park** the **car**

7. **start** the **car**
   It was **hard** to **start** the **car.**
8. **wants** to **operate**
   The **doctor wants** to **operate.**
9. **solve problems**
   Honest politicians solve problems.
10. **watch stopped**
    My **watch stopped** at five **o'clock.**
11. **shot** in the **dark**
    Don heard a **shot** in the **dark.**
12. **park** the **car**
    Did **father park** the **car?**

13. **forgot** to **lock**
    I **forgot** to **lock** the **apartment.**
14. **shop** for **bargains**
    Barbara wants to **shop** for **bargains.**
15. **top-notch***
    The **top-notch marksman**† shot the **target.**

 SELF-TEST I   (Correct answers may be found in Appendix II on page 168.)

Listen carefully as the teacher or the instructor on the tape presents ten three-word series. Circle the number of the **ONE** word in each series that is pronounced with [a].

EXAMPLE: The instructor says: not   note   nut
                   You circle: ①   2   3

1. 1 2 3	6. 1 2 3	
2. 1 2 3	7. 1 2 3	
3. 1 2 3.	8. 1 2 3·	
4. 1 2 3	9. 1 2· 3	
5. 1 2 3	10. 1 2· 3	

SELF-TEST II   (Correct answers may be found in Appendix II on page 168.)

In English, the names of the following places all have the vowel [a]. Circle the vowel in each *"far off place"* that should be pronounced [a] **when speaking English. This exercise is not on the tape.**

EXAMPLES: a. L a P@z
                   b. St©ckholm

1. Vermont
2. Moscow
3. Bahamas
4. Scotland
5. Nevada

6. Holland
7. Morocco
8. Caracas
9. Chicago
10. Oslo

*top-notch = superior

†marksman = tirador

42   [a] as in ARM

You are a photographer for a well known magazine! Your assignment is to photograph animals whose names contain the vowel [a]*.* Repeat the names of the following "creatures" after your teacher or the instructor on the tape. Circle only animals pronounced with [a].

(condor)	(collie)	leopard	llama
cat	crocodile	elephant	sea otter
fox	tiger	hippopotamus	dolphin
iguana	kangaroo	lobster	octopus
parrot	rhinoceros	opossum	lion

SELF-TEST IV   (Correct answers may be found in Appendix II on page 168.)

Read the following paragraph on the *Constitution* aloud. Circle all words that should be pronounced with the [a] vowel. **This self-test is not on the tape.**

. . . .

The (Constitution)

The United States Constitution is the basis of our democracy. Much compromise was necessary before the constitution was adopted. Some modifications to the constitution caused problems which were resolved by forming two houses in Congress. Other countries change their constitutions when a new politician takes office. The United States Constitution has been constant but responsive to change. We thank our founding fathers for this remarkable document.

. . . .

After checking your answers in Appendix II, practice reading the paragraph again. Remember to open your mouth wide and **"yawn"** as you pronounce the [a] vowel!

FOR AN ENCORE ....

Listening

Listen to your favorite newscaster on radio or TV. Specifically listen for all the words pronounced with [a]. List as many as you can in a period of three minutes. Practice your list of [a] words aloud.

COMPLETE ALL THE ACTIVITIES AND ....

⟨⟨⟨ *WE'RE POSITIVE YOU'LL BE ON TARGET WITH* [a] ⟩⟩⟩

```
*********************************************
```

REVIEW OF [eɪ] [ɛ] [æ] AND [a]

```
*********************************************
```

JAW LOWERS (mouth opens)

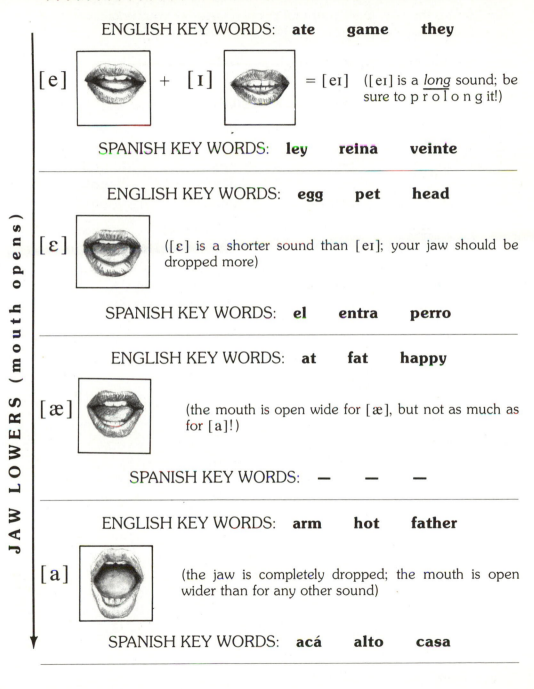

ENGLISH KEY WORDS: **ate   game   they**

[e] **+** [ɪ] **=** [eɪ]   ([eɪ] is a *long* sound; be sure to p r o l o n g it!)

SPANISH KEY WORDS: **ley   reina   veinte**

ENGLISH KEY WORDS: **egg   pet   head**

[ɛ]   ([ɛ] is a shorter sound than [eɪ]; your jaw should be dropped more)

SPANISH KEY WORDS: **el   entra   perro**

ENGLISH KEY WORDS: **at   fat   happy**

[æ]   (the mouth is open wide for [æ], but not as much as for [a]!)

SPANISH KEY WORDS: —   —   —

ENGLISH KEY WORDS: **arm   hot   father**

[a]   (the jaw is completely dropped; the mouth is open wider than for any other sound)

SPANISH KEY WORDS: **acá   alto   casa**

REVIEW EXERCISE

Repeat the rows of words and sentences accurately after your teacher or the instructor on the tape. Feel your mouth open wider as you progress through the pronunciation of the [eɪ] [ɛ] [æ] and [a] words.

MOUTH OPENS WIDER ⟶

[eɪ]	[ɛ]	[æ]	[a]
1. *ai*d	*E*d	*a*dd	*o*dd
2. r*a*ke	wr*e*ck	r*a*ck	r*o*ck
3. p*ai*d	p*e*d	p*a*d	p*o*d
4. N*a*te	n*e*t	gn*a*t*	n*o*t
5. p*ai*ned	p*e*nned	p*a*nned	p*o*nd

6. I had a **rake**.   I had a **wreck**.   I had a **rack**.   I had a **rock**.
7. Can you **tape** it?   Can you **tap** it?   Can you **top** it?
8. Do you know **Jane**?   Do you know **Jan**?   Do you know **John**?
9. The **paste** is gone.   The **pest** is gone.   The **past** is gone.
10. He took the **bait**.   He took the **bet**.   He took the **bat**.

11. I h**a**te wearing a h**a**t when it's h**o**t.
    [eɪ]   [æ]   [a]
12. The house at the l**a**ke l**a**cks a l**o**ck.
                   [eɪ] [æ]   [a]
13. R**o**n r**a**n in the r**ai**n.
    [a] [æ]   [eɪ]
14. It's **o**dd that **E**d can't **a**dd.
      [a]   [ɛ]   [æ]
15. D**a**n, the gr**ea**t d**a**ne, sleeps in the d**e**n.
    [æ]   [eɪ]   [eɪ]   [ɛ]

*gnat = cénzalo

Your teacher or the instructor on the tape will present the following sentences using **ONE** of the words in parentheses. Listen carefully and circle the word (and vowel) used.

EXAMPLE: I'll write that   (letter   later).
                                    [ɛ]   [eɪ]

1. Leave the car in the   (shed   shade).
                              [ɛ]   [eɪ] ·

2. Do you know what was   (sad   said)?
                              [æ]   [ɛ] ·

3. We need more   (paper   pepper).
                       [eɪ] ·   [ɛ]

4. Please clear that   (debt   date).
                           [ɛ]   [eɪ] ·

5. Children like   (pets   pats).
                       [ɛ] ·   [æ]

6. They made the   (plan   plane).
                        [æ]   [eɪ] ·

7. I bought a new   (pen   pan).
                        [ɛ] ·   [æ]

8. The note is in the   (packet   pocket).
                            [æ]   [a] ·

9. Did she pay for the   (band   bond)?
                             [æ]   [a] ·

10. I think it was   (odd   Ed).
                        [a] ·   [ɛ]

Now that you have completed the review test, read each of the sentences twice. Carefully pronounce the first word in parentheses in the first reading and the contrast word in the second reading.

(Correct answers may be found in Appendix II on page 169.)

Read the following words aloud. Write each word under the symbol that represents the vowel sound of the boldface letter(s). **This review test is not on the tape.**

m**a**tch	fr**ei**ght	w**a**tch	bl**o**nde	**A**pril
sh**o**ck	p**a**rt	v**a**st	f**o**x	**a**pple
pl**a**ne	h**a**lf	**e**gg	c**a**n't	t**o**p
b**e**ll	st**ea**k	l**au**gh	pl**ai**d	st**a**ple
g**ue**ss	**a**ny	v**ei**l	s**ai**d	h**e**lp
w**a**sp	n**a**me	fr**ie**nd	**ai**d	st**o**p

[eɪ] as in *ATE*	[ɛ] as in *EGG*	[æ] as in *HAT*	[a] as in *HOT*

After checking your answers in Appendix II, carefully pronounce all of the above words again.

REVIEW TEST III

(Correct answers may be found in Appendix II on page 169.)

Listen carefully to your teacher or the tape as ten sentences are presented. One word in each sentence will be **incorrectly** pronounced. On the line to the right of each number, write the **CORRECT** word for the sentence.

Sentence #   **Correct Word**

EXAMPLE a: _____wet_____   (I got **wait** in the rain.)

EXAMPLE b: _____bait_____   (The fisherman needed **bat**.)

1.   _____

2.   _____slede_____

3.   _____headach._____

4.   _____watch_____

5.   _____late_____

6.   _____

7.   _____pet_____

8.   _____cat_____

9.   _____tastes_____

10.   _____weight_____

In the brackets provided, write the number of the phonetic symbol representing the vowel sound of the underlined letter(s). Then identify the person
described in each paragraph. **This review test is not on the tape.**

Pronunciation Key: 1 = [eɪ] as in *NAME*   3 = [æ] as in *HAT*
2 = [ɛ] as in *BET*   4 = [a] as in *HOT*

. . . .

[1]   [2]   [ ]   [ ]
He was a famous president of the United States. He was elected in
[ ]   [ ] [ ]   [ ]   [ ]
eighteen sixty. He was known as Honest Abe. He freed the slaves. The name
[ ]
of this man is ———————— .

. . . .

[ ]   [ ]   [ ]   [ ]
She was a famous queen. She reigned in Spain and married Ferdinand.
[ ]   [ ]   [ ]   [ ]   [ ]
She sent Columbus to a large new continent. This voyage started the settle-
[ ]   [ ]   [ ]
ment of America. The name of this lady is ———————— .

. . . .

[ ]   [ ]   [ ]   [ ]
He was a famous playwright. He came from England and is probably the
[ ]   [ ]   [ ] [ ]   [ ]
most popular writer in the world. His dramas have been translated into every
[ ]   [ ]   [ ]   [ ]   [ ]   [ ]
language. Shylock, Macbeth, and Henry VI are among his many characters.
[ ]   [ ]
The name of this man is ———————— .

. . . .

```
*****************************************************
```

[u] as in *YOU TOO* and *RULE*

⟨DICTIONARY MARK: o͞o⟩

AND

[ʊ] as in *COOK* and *PUT*

⟨DICTIONARY MARK: *oo or* o͝o⟩

```
*****************************************************
```

PRONOUNCING [u]

LIPS:	are tense and in a "whistling" position.
JAW:	is completely raised.
TONGUE:	is high near the roof of the mouth.

The sound [u] in English is similar to stressed "ú" in Spanish. ([u] is actually more prolonged than Spanish "ú".)

SPANISH KEY WORDS WITH [u]

Spanish words with this sound are spelled with "u" or "ú".

> **KEY WORDS:** *su   luna   jugo   "mucho gusto"*

POSSIBLE PRONUNCIATION PROBLEMS
FOR THE SPANISH SPEAKER

Pronunciation problems occur because of confusing English spelling patterns and the similarity of [u] and [ʊ] (the sound to be described next).

EXAMPLES: When you substitute [ʊ] for [u]:   *pool* becomes ***pull***
suit becomes ***soot***

YOU CAN DO IT! You already produce the* [u] *vowel in Spanish. Your lips should be tense and in a "whistling" position.* [u] *is a LONG sound; be sure to p r o l o n g it. If you remember to PROTRUDE your lips when PRODUCING* [u], *YOU'LL never CONFUSE "pull" with "POOL"!!!

EXERCISE A

The following words should all be pronounced with [u]. Repeat them carefully after your teacher or the instructor on the tape.*

[u] **In the Middle**	[u] **At the End**
food	do
pool	new
room	you
suit	shoe
truth	flew
goose	chew
group	threw
ruler	through
school	canoe

[u] **spelled:**

"u"	"oo"	"o"	"ew"	"ue"
rule	cool	do	new	due
rude	fool	to	drew	blue
June	too	who	stew	clue
tune	noon	tomb	knew	glued
tuna	stool	lose	news	avenue

> **NOTE:** When the letter "u" follows "t", "d", "n", or "s", some Americans pronounce it [ju].
>
> EXAMPLES: Tuesday duty new suit

Less frequent spelling patterns for [u] consist of the letters "ui", "ou", "oe", "ieu", and "ough".

EXAMPLES: fr**ui**t gr**ou**p sh**oe** l**ieu**tenant thr**ough**

*The vowel [u] does not occur at the beginning of words in English.

EXERCISE B

Read the following pairs of [u] words aloud. **PROLONG** the vowel [u] before the consonant. (The dots are there to remind you to p r o l o n g the [u].) **This exercise is not on the tape.**

1. new   new . . . . s   (news)
2. due   due . . . . s   (dues)
3. sue   sue . . . . d   (sued)
4. who   who . . . . m   (whom)
5. glue   glue . . . . d   (glued)

EXERCISE C

The boldface words in the following phrases and sentences should all be pronounced with the vowel [u]. Repeat them carefully after your teacher or the instructor on the tape.

1. What's **new**?
2. **Who** is it?
3. How are **you**?
4. **loose tooth**
5. in the **mood**

6. **School** will **soon** be **through**.
7. **You** must **chew** your **food**.
8. He **proved** he **knew** the **truth**.
9. The **group flew to New** York.
10. **Who ruined** my **new shoes**?
11. The **rude students** broke the **rules**.
12. It's **too cool to use** the **pool**.
13. **Do you** prefer **soup** or **stew**?
14. The **beautiful tulips** are **blooming**.
15. I'm not in the **mood** for **Sue's stupid humor**!

 SELF-TEST I   (Correct answers may be found in Appendix II on page 170.)

Listen carefully to your teacher or the tape as ten three-word series are presented. **ONE** word in each group will be pronounced with [u]. Circle the number of the word with the vowel [u].

EXAMPLE: The instructor says: comb   cool   call
            You circle: 1   ②   3

1. 1 2 3·   6. 1· 2 3
2. 1 2 3   7. 1· 2 3
3. 1· 2 3   8. 1 2· 3
4. 1· 2 3   9. 1 2 3·
5. 1 2 3   10. 1 2· 3

PRONOUNCING [ʊ]

LIPS:	are relaxed and slightly parted.
JAW:	is slightly lower than for [u].
TONGUE:	is high, but lower than for [u].

POSSIBLE PRONUNCIATION PROBLEMS FOR THE SPANISH SPEAKER

The vowel [ʊ] doesn't exist in Spanish and may be difficult for you to hear and produce. You probably substitute the more familiar [u] sound.

EXAMPLES: When you substitute [u] for [ʊ]: ***full***   sounds like   ***fool***
                                     cook   sounds like   ***kook****

As you repeat the exercise words, remember NOT to protrude your lips and tense them as you would for [u]. [ʊ] **is a SHORT, QUICK sound; your lips should barely move while saying it.** *Practice* [ʊ] *as you* ***SHO̲U̲LD, and you'll be UNDERST̲O̲O̲D!!!***

EXERCISE A

The following words should all be pronounced with [ʊ]. Repeat them carefully after your teacher or the instructor on the tape.† (***RELAX*** your lips and jaw as you produce [ʊ].)

[ʊ] In the Middle

cook	put
full	wood
book	took
good	foot
stood	brook
look	hood
shook	sugar
push	woman
could	cushion

*kook = persona alocada o excéntrica

†The vowel [ʊ] is found only in the middle of words.

[ʊ] spelled:

"u"	"oo"	"ou"
pull	wool	could
put	wood	would
push	hook	should
bullet	good	
pudding	cookie	

A less frequent spelling pattern for [ʊ] is the letter "o".

EXAMPLES: w**o**lf   w**o**man

HINTS: a. The letters "oo" followed by "d" or "k" are usually pronounced [ʊ].

   EXAMPLES: h**oo**d   g**oo**d   w**oo**d   b**oo**k   l**oo**k   c**oo**k

   b. The letter "u" followed by "sh" is usually pronounced [ʊ].

   EXAMPLES: b**ush**   p**ush**   c**ush**ion

 EXERCISE B

The boldface words in the following phrases and sentences should all be pronounced with the [ʊ] vowel. Repeat them carefully after your teacher or the instructor on the tape.

1. **Look** out!
2. Take a **good look**.
3. **good-looking**
4. He **couldn't** come.
5. **Should** we go?

6. Who **took** my **book**?
7. **Put** the **wood** away.
8. He **took** a **look** at the **crook**.
9. The **woman stood** on one **foot**.
10. **Could** you eat ten **sugar cookies**?
11. The **woods** are **full** of **bushes**.
12. The **butcher should** be a **good cook**.
13. He **couldn't pull** the **wool** over my eyes!
14. The hunter **looked** for the **wolf** in the **woods**.
15. In Pamplona, men **push** and **pull** the **bulls**!

SELF-TEST I (Correct answers may be found in Appendix II on page 170.)

Listen carefully as your teacher or the instructor on the tape presents ten sentences. Some words that should be pronounced with [ʊ] will be said INCORRECTLY. Circle **"C"** for **CORRECT** or **"I"** for **INCORRECT** to indicate whether the [ʊ] word in each sentence is pronounced properly.

Sentence #	Response	
EXAMPLE:	C (I)	(I was **fool** after eating.)
EXAMPLE:	(C) I	(The **cushion** is soft.)
1.	C I	
2.	C I	
3.	C I	
4.	C I	
5.	C I	
6.	C I	
7.	C I	
8.	C I	
9.	C I	
10.	C I	

```
*********************************************
```

REVIEW OF [u] and [ʊ]

```
*********************************************
```

▶ ORAL EXERCISE

Repeat the pairs of words and sentences carefully after your teacher or the instructor on the tape. REMEMBER to feel tension and **PROTRUDE** your lips when you repeat the words with [u] and to **RELAX** your muscles as you pronounce the [ʊ] words.

[u]	[ʊ]
1. fool	full
2. suit	soot
3. Luke	look
4. pool	pull
5. stewed	stood

6. I hate the black **suit**.   I hate the black **soot**.
7. She went to **Luke**.   She went to **look**.
8. I have no **pool**.   I have no **pull**.
9. He's quite a **kook**!   He's quite a **cook**!
10. The beef **stewed** for an hour.   The beef **stood** for an hour.

11. Take a **good look** at **Luke**.
       [ʊ]   [ʊ]   [u]

12. **Pull** him from the **pool**.
       [ʊ]   [u]

13. He has **soot** on his **suit**.
       [ʊ]   [u]

14. The **fool** was **full** of fun.
       [u]   [ʊ]

15. The horse **should** be **shoed**.
         [ʊ]   [u]

SELF-TEST I   (Correct answers may be found in Appendix II on page 171.)

Your teacher or the instructor on the tape will say only **ONE** word in each of the following pairs. Listen carefully and circle the word that you hear.

EXAMPLES: a. pooled   (pulled)
                    b. (kooky)   cookie

[u]	[ʊ]
1. cooed*	could
2. who'd	hood
3. stewed	stood
4. pool	pull
5. shoed	should
6. fool	full
7. wooed†	would
8. Luke	look
9. kook	cook
10. suit	soot‡

SELF-TEST II   (Correct answers may be found in Appendix II on page 171.)

Listen carefully to your teacher or the tape as ten three-word series are presented. Two of the words in each group will be the SAME; one will be DIFFERENT. Circle the number of the word that is **different**.

EXAMPLE: The instructor says: should   should   shoed
                       You circle: 1   2   ③

1.	1 2 3		6.	1 2 3	
2.	1 2 3		7.	① 2 3	
3.	1 2 3		8.	1 2 3	
4.	1 2 3		9.	① 2 3	
5.	1 2 3		10.	① 2 3	

*coo = arrullar
†woo = cortejar
‡soot = hollín

SELF-TEST III (Correct answers may be found in Appendix II on page 171.)

Read each of the following sentences aloud. On the line above each italicized word, write the phonetic symbol ([u] or [ʊ]) representing the vowel in that word. **This self-test is not on the tape.**

EXAMPLE:
[ʊ]   [u]
Pull the raft from the ***pool***.

1. [ ]   [ ]   [ ]
Too many ***cooks*** spoil the ***soup***!

2. [ ]   [ ] [ ]
There ***should*** be a ***full moon***.

3. [ ]   [ ] [ ]
Mr. ***Brooks*** is ***good looking***.

4. [ ]   [ ]   [ ]
June is a ***good*** month to ***move***.

5. [ ]   [ ]   [ ]
The ***butcher cooked*** a ***goose***.

6. [ ] [ ]   [ ]
The ***news bulletin*** was ***misunderstood***.

7. [ ] [ ]   [ ] [ ]
Did ***you choose*** a pair of ***new shoes***?

8. [ ]   [ ] [ ] [ ]
Lucy had a ***loose tooth pulled***.

9. [ ]   [ ]   [ ] [ ]
Students should read ***good books***.

10. [ ]   [ ]   [ ]   [ ]
The ***room*** is ***full*** of ***blue balloons***.

Listen carefully to your teacher or the tape as the following paragraph about *Harry Houdini* is read. **CIRCLE** all words pronounced with [u] and **UNDERLINE** all words pronounced with [ʊ].

· ·

Harry (Houdini) was a magician known (throughout) the world. He could remove himself from chains and ropes and could walk through walls! Houdini was born in Budapest, Hungary. He moved to New York when he was twelve and soon took up magic. Rumors spread that Houdini had supernatural pow-ers. However, he was truthful and stated that his tricks could be understood by all humans! Houdini is an idol* for all would-be† magicians.

· ·

After checking your answers in Appendix II, practice reading the paragraph aloud. **REMEMBER—*your lips must be in a TENSE "whistling" posi-tion for* [u] *and RELAXED when pronouncing* [ʊ].**

FOR AN ENCORE ·

Reading

Read one or two headline news stories on the front page of the newspaper. Circle all [ʊ] and [u] words. Read the sentences containing the circled words aloud. Carefully pronounce the [ʊ] and [u] vowel sounds.

PRACTICE [u] AND [u] AS YOU SHOULD AND · · · · · · · · · · · · · · · · · ·

⟨⟨⟨ *YOU WILL BE UNDERSTOOD* ⟩⟩⟩

*idol = ídolo
†would-be = aspirante

```
*****************************************************
```

[ʌ] as in *UP BUT* and *COME*

⟨DICTIONARY MARK: u *or* ŭ⟩

```
*****************************************************
```

PRONOUNCING [ʌ]

LIPS:	are relaxed and slightly parted.
JAW:	is relaxed and slightly lowered.
TONGUE:	is relaxed and midlevel in the mouth.

POSSIBLE PRONUNCIATION PROBLEMS
FOR THE SPANISH SPEAKER

The vowel [ʌ] does not exist in Spanish and may be difficult for you to hear and pronounce. It is easy to become confused by irregular English spelling patterns and to substitute sounds that are more familiar to you.

EXAMPLES: If you say [a] instead of [ʌ]: *color* will sound like *collar*
If you say [ʊ] instead of [ʌ]: *come* will sound like *comb*
If you say [ɔ] instead of [ʌ]: *done* will sound like *dawn*

Remember, [ʌ] is a short, quick sound. You shouldn't feel any tension and your lips should barely move during its production. *J<u>U</u>ST relax as you say [ʌ] and you won't R<u>U</u>N into TRO<u>U</u>BLE!!!*

 **EXERCISE A**

The following words should all be pronounced with the [ʌ] vowel. Repeat them accurately after your teacher or the instructor on the tape.*

[ʌ] **At the Beginning**	[ʌ] **In the Middle**
us	hug
up	won
of	nut
oven	does
ugly	much
other	must
usher	come
under	rough
uncle	month
onion	trouble

[ʌ] **spelled:**

"u"	**"o"**
but	love
cut	done
sun	some
lucky	mother
funny	Monday

Less frequent spelling patterns for [ʌ] consist of the letters "ou", "oo", "oe", and "a".

EXAMPLES: **cou**sin tr**ou**ble fl**oo**d d**oe**s w**a**s wh**a**t

---

*The vowel [ʌ] does not occur at the end of words in English.

EXERCISE B

Repeat the following pairs of words after your teacher or the instructor on the tape. When repeating the words with [ʌ], your lips must be completely relaxed and should barely move.

[ʌ]	[a]
cut	cot
luck	lock
come	calm
wonder	wander
color	collar
hut	hot
nut	not
bum	bomb
pup	pop
fund	fond

*Refer to page 94 for a complete description of the unstressed vowel [ə].

The boldface words in the following phrases and sentences should all be pronounced with the vowel [ʌ]. Repeat them accurately after your teacher or the instructor on the tape.

1. **Come** in.
2. **What does** it mean?
3. **bubble gum**

4. **once** a **month**
5. **once** is **enough**
6. **cover up**

7. **mother's brother**
   My **uncle** is my **mother's brother.**
8. **uncle's son**
   My **cousin** is my **uncle's son.**
9. **ugly color**
   The **gloves** are **such** an **ugly color.**
10. **fun** in the **sun**
    Come have **some fun** in the **sun.**
11. **summer months**
    I **love** the **summer months** in the **country.**
12. **lucky couple**
    The **lucky couple won some money.**
13. **under** the **rug**
    Never sweep **dust under** the **rug.**
14. **comes from**
    Does Bud's cousin come from London?
15. **sucks** his **thumb**
    My **young son sucks** his **thumb.**

Read the following *"lunch menu"* aloud. Select your *"lunch"* by circling the foods pronounced with the [ʌ] vowel. **This self-test is not on the tape.**

COCKTAILS
Martini   Wine   (Rum Punch)

APPETIZERS
Stuffed Mushrooms   Shrimp Cocktail   Melon

SOUPS
Gazpacho   French Onion   Clam Chowder

SALAD
Hearts of Lettuce   Caesar   Tomato and Cucumber

VEGETABLES
Buttered Corn   Baked Potato   Carrots

ENTREES
Arroz con Pollo   Prime Ribs   Roast Duck

BREADS
Italian Bread   Hot Muffins   Garlic Rolls

DESSERTS
Pumpkin Pie   Vanilla Pudding   Ice Cream

BEVERAGES
Coffee   Milk   Cup of Tea

. . . .

After checking your answers in the Appendix, practice **each** circled menu item by saying it in the sentence *"I had _____ for lunch."*

EXAMPLE: **"I had** (a) ***rum punch* for lunch."**

Remember to pronounce all the [ʌ] *"lunch items"* carefully!

SELF-TEST II   (Correct answers may be found in Appendix II on page 172.)

Listen carefully as your teacher or instructor on the tape presents ten sentences. Some words that should be pronounced with [ʌ] will be said INCORRECTLY. Circle **"C"** for **Correct** or **"I"** for **Incorrect** to indicate whether the [ʌ] word in each sentence is pronounced properly.

EXAMPLE: Ⓒ   I   (I **love** to watch children play.)
EXAMPLE: C   Ⓘ   (The heavy bricks weigh a **tone**.)

1.   C   I
2.   C   I
3.   C   I
4.   C   I
5.   C   I
6.   C   I
7.   C   I
8.   C   I
9.   C   I
10.   C   I

SELF-TEST III   (Correct answers may be found in Appendix II on page 172.)

Listen carefully to your teacher or the tape as ten four-word series are presented. Circle the **ONE** word in each group of four that is **NOT** pronounced with [ʌ].

EXAMPLE: once   lovely   (alone)   funny

1. something   wonder   ugly   open
2. trouble   come   locker   once
3. color   cups   dozen   collar
4. peanut   muddy   modern   bunny
5. stood   stuff   stump   stuck
6. lucky   brother   just   lock
7. Monday   month   Tuesday   Sunday
8. comb   coming   cutting   country
9. cover   over   oven   other
10. rust   must   rot   nothing

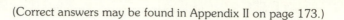

Listen carefully to your teacher or the tape as the following dialogue is read. Circle all the words pronounced with the vowel [ʌ].

. . . .

GUS: Hi **Russ**! How's my *fun loving buddy*?
RUSSELL: Very worried. I just had a run of tough luck.*
GUS: Why, what's up?
RUSSELL: My bus got stuck in the mud and I lost some money. I should carry something for luck!
GUS: Yes. Here's some other advice. Never walk under ladders, and run from black cats. They're nothing but trouble!
RUSSELL: Oh, Gus. You must be a nut! Do you really believe such "mumbo jumbo"?†
GUS: Don't make fun, Russ. Such customs come from many countries. You must know others!
RUSSELL: Well, the number 13 is unlucky. And, a blister on the tongue means someone is lying!
GUS: Right! But—you can have good luck too. Discover a four-leaf clover, or find bubbles in your coffee cup and you'll get a sum of money.
RUSSELL: OK, Gus. Maybe I'll have some luck this month. *Knock on wood!!!*

. . . .

After checking your answers in Appendix II, practice the dialogue out loud with a friend. Carefully pronounce all [ʌ] words.

MAY THE GOOD <u>LUCK</u> BE YOURS!!!

FOR AN ENCORE . . . .

Listening

The theme of many popular songs today is **"LOVE."** Listen to your favorite radio station, record album, or tape. Select a "love" song and make a list of all the [ʌ] words you hear. After the song is over, practice your list of words aloud. Be sure to say the word ***"love"*** correctly. This activity can be done alone if you prefer!

JUST RELAX AS YOU SAY [ʌ] AND . . . .

⟨⟨⟨ *YOU WON'T R<u>U</u>N INTO TRO<u>U</u>BLE WITH* [<u>ʌ</u>] ⟩⟩⟩

*tough luck = mala suerte   †mumbo jumbo = tonterías

68   [ʌ] as in UP

```
********************************************
```

[OU] as in *OH NO* and *BOAT*

⟨DICTIONARY MARK: ō⟩

```
********************************************
```

PRONOUNCING [ou]

 +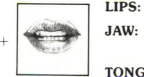

LIPS:	are tense and very round.
JAW:	rises with the tongue and closes slightly.
TONGUE:	glides from midlevel to near the roof of the mouth.

[ou] is a diphthong. It begins with [o] and ends with [u].

[ou] in English is similar to stressed "ó" in Spanish. ([ou] is actually longer and more prolonged than Spanish "ó".)

SPANISH KEY WORDS WITH [ou]

Spanish words with this sound are spelled with "o" or "ó".

KEY WORDS:* *no*   *cosa*   *dólar*   *habló*

POSSIBLE PRONUNCIATION PROBLEMS FOR THE SPANISH SPEAKER

Once again your pronunciation problems with this sound occur because of confusing English spelling patterns and the similarities between other vowel sounds.

EXAMPLES: If you substitute [ʌ] for [ou]:   ***coat*** will sound like ***cut***
            If you substitute [ɔ] for [ou]:   ***bold*** will sound like ***bald***

When producing the diphthong [ou] round your lips into the shape of the letter "o"! [ou] is a **LONG** sound; be sure to prolong it. Listen carefully to your teacher or the tapes and ***your*** [o͟u] ***will be O͟K!!!***

---

*The uncommon Spanish word "bou" actually contains the prolonged diphthong [ou].

The following words should all be pronounced with [ou]. Repeat them carefully after your teacher or the instructor on the tape.

[ou] **At the Beginning**	[ou] **In the Middle**	[ou] **At the End**
oat	boat	go
own	both	so
oak	coat	no
old	nose	toe
omen	roam	sew
only	loan	ago
over	known	show
oval	spoke	snow
open	soul	hello
ocean	don't	though

[ou] **spelled:**

"o"	**"oa"**	**"ow"**	**"oe"**	**"ou"**
no	soap	know	toe	dough
rope	goat	owe	foe	though
vote	loan	grow	goes	shoulder
home	foam	throw		
fold	load	bowl		

HINTS: a. When "o" is in a syllable ending in silent "e", the letter "o" is pronounced [ou] (the same name as the alphabet letter "O"!!!).

EXAMPLES: ph**o**ne n**o**te h**o**me r**o**pe

b. The letters "oa" are usually pronounced [ou].

EXAMPLES: c**oa**l b**oa**t r**oa**sting t**oa**ster

c. The letter "o" followed by "ld" is usually pronounced [ou].

EXAMPLES: c**old** **old** s**old**ier t**old**

EXERCISE B

Read the following pairs of [ou] words aloud. **P R O L O N G** the diphthong [ou] before the consonant. (The dots are there to remind you to **p r o- l o n g** the [ou].) **This exercise is not on the tape.**

1. toe   toe . . . . s   (toes)
2. sew   sew . . . . s   (sews)
3. grow   grow . . . . . . s   (grows)
4. know   know . . . . . n   (known)
5. blow   blow . . . . . . n   (blown)

 ## EXERCISE C

Repeat the following pairs of words after your teacher or the instructor on the tape. Be sure to **P R O L O N G** the diphthong [ou].

[ou]	[ʌ]
phone	fun
bone	bun
roam	rum
boast	bust
tone	ton
coat	cut
boat	but
hole	hull
comb	come
most	must

EXERCISE D

The boldface words in the following phrases and sentences should all be pronounced with the diphthong [ou]. Repeat them carefully after your teacher or the instructor on the tape.

1. Leave me **alone**!
2. I **suppose so**.
3. **over** and **over**

4. **hold** the **phone**
5. **open** and **close**
6. at a **moment's notice**

7. **broke** his **toe**
   Tony broke his **toe**.
8. **own clothes**
   I **sew** my **own clothes**.
9. **homegrown**
   The **tomatoes** are **homegrown**.
10. **don't go**
    Don't go home so soon.
11. **gold sold**
    Gold sold at a **low** price.
12. **below zero**
    It was **below zero** in **Oklahoma**.
13. **only joking**
    I **hope** you're **only joking**!
14. **over** and **over**
    Repeat the [ou] words **over** and **over**!
15. **no** one **knows**
    How **old** is **Flo**? **No** one **knows**!

Read the following list of **"household"** items out loud. (The items pronounced with [ou] are broken. You need to fix them!) Circle **ONLY** the broken [ou] items. **This self-test is not on the tape.**

(toaster)	frying pan	bookcase	freezer
clock	telephone	faucet	radio
stove	sofa	lawn mower	table
doorknob	window	television	coat rack
can opener	mixing bowl	clothes dryer	iron

After checking your answers in Appendix II, practice each **broken [ou] item by saying it in the sentence,** "The _____ is **broken.**"

EXAMPLE: "The **toaster** is **broken.**"

SELF-TEST II   (Correct answers may be found in Appendix II on page 173.)

Listen carefully to your teacher or the tape as ten pairs of sentences are presented. Circle **"SAME"** if both the sentences in each pair are the **same.** If they are **NOT** the same, circle **"DIFFERENT."**

Pair #   **Response**

EXAMPLE a: same (different) (It was **slaw.** It was **slow.**)
EXAMPLE b: (same) different   (I have a **cut.** I have a **cut.**)

1.	same	different
2.	same	different
3.	same	different
4.	same	different
5.	same	different
6.	same	different
7.	same	different
8.	same	different
9.	same	different
10.	same	different

SELF-TEST III   (Correct answers may be found in Appendix II on page 174.)

Read each four-word series aloud. (Only **ONE** word in each group has the diphthong [ou].) Circle the **ONE** word in each series that **IS** pronounced with [ou]. **This self-test is not on the tape.**

EXAMPLE: milk   root beer   punch   (coke)

1. brown	towel	known	crowd
2. trouble	notice	normal	pocket
3. orange	carrot	yellow	lemon
4. foot	toes	ankle	eyebrow
5. politics	office	vote	governor
6. comb	tomb	bomb	come
7. essay	poem	story	book
8. prove	love	stove	shove
9. world	town	country	road
10. tomato	olive	corn	onion

SELF-TEST IV   (Correct answers may be found in Appendix II on page 174.)

Listen carefully to your teacher or the tape as the following dialogue is read. Circle all the words pronounced with [ou].

. . . .

JOE: (Rosa) let's (go) on a trip. We need to be (alone)
ROSA: OK, Joe. Where should we go?
JOE: I know! We'll go to Ohio.
ROSA: Great! We'll visit my Uncle Roland.
JOE: No, it's too cold in Ohio. We'll go to Arizona.
ROSA: Fine. We'll stay with your Aunt Mona!
JOE: No, it's too hot in Arizona. Let's go to Rome.
ROSA: Oh, good! You'll meet my Cousin Tony.
JOE: No, no, no!! We won't go to Rome. Let's go to Nome, Alaska. We don't know anyone there!!
ROSA: You won't believe it, but I have an old friend . . . . .
JOE: Hold it, Rosa, We won't go anywhere! I suppose we'll just stay home.

. . . .

After checking your answers in Appendix II, practice the dialogue out loud with a friend. **P r o l o n g** all [ou] words!

FOR AN ENCORE ....

Reading

Look at a map of the United States. Find as many cities and states as you can that are pronounced with [oʊ]. Practice saying their names aloud.

PRACTICE [oʊ] OVER AND OVER!!!

⟨⟨⟨ *YOUR* [o] *WILL BE OK* ⟩⟩⟩

```
*********************************************
```

[ɔ] as in *ALL CAUGHT* and *BOSS*

⟨DICTIONARY MARK: ô⟩

```
*********************************************
```

PRONOUNCING [ɔ]

LIPS:	are in a tense oval shape and slightly protruded.
JAW:	is open more than for [ou].
TONGUE:	is low near the floor of the mouth.

POSSIBLE PRONUNCIATION PROBLEMS
FOR THE SPANISH SPEAKER

The vowel [ɔ] is another *"trouble maker"* that doesn't exist in Spanish! Confusing English spelling patterns frequently make you substitute more familiar vowels.

EXAMPLES: If you substitute [a] for [ɔ]: ***caller*** will become ***collar***
If you substitute [ou] for [ɔ]: ***bought*** will become ***boat***
If you substitute [ʌ] for [ɔ]: ***bought*** will become ***but***

As you listen to your teacher or the tapes, your pronunciation of [ɔ] will improve. **Remember to protrude *YOUR* lips and drop *YOUR JAW* when you say [ɔ]!**

EXERCISE A

The following words should all be pronounced with the [ɔ] vowel. Repeat them accurately after your teacher or the instructor on the tape.

[ɔ] **At the Beginning**	[ɔ] **In the Middle**	[ɔ] **At the End**
or	boss	awe
all	fall	raw
off	song	law
also	store	saw
awful	wrong	flaw
often	broad	draw
ought	bought	claw
always	taught	thaw
August	across	straw
audience	naughty	

[ɔ] **spelled:**

"o"	**"a"**	**"aw"**	**"au"**
dog	fall	jaw	auto
toss	call	lawn	fault
lost	mall	dawn	cause
long	salt	drawn	pauper
offer	stall	awful	auction

Less frequent spelling patterns for [ɔ] consist of the letters "oa" and "ou".

EXAMPLES: br**oa**d c**ou**gh th**ou**ght

> **HINTS:** a. The letter "o" followed by "ff", "ng", and "ss" is usually pronounced [ɔ].
>
> EXAMPLES: **off**er **off** l**ong** str**ong** l**oss** t**oss**ing
>
> b. The letters "aw" are usually pronounced [ɔ].
>
> EXAMPLES: l**aw**n dr**aw aw**ful
>
> c. The letter "a" followed by "ll", "lk", "lt", and "ld" is usually pronounced [ɔ].
>
> EXAMPLES: b**all** t**alk** s**alt** b**ald**

EXERCISE B

Repeat the following pairs of words after your teacher or the instructor on the tape. When repeating the [ɔ] words, be sure to protrude your lips **more** than for the other sounds.

I		II		III	
[ɔ]	**[ʌ]**	**[ɔ]**	**[ou]**	**[ɔ]**	**[a]**
dog	dug	saw	so	for	far
dawn	done	law	low	stalk	stock
long	lung	tall	toll	taught	tot
cough	cuff	bald	bold	caught	cot
bought	but	bought	boat	caller	collar

EXERCISE C

The boldface words in the following phrases and questions/answers should all be pronounced with the vowel [ɔ]. Repeat them carefully after your teacher or the instructor on the tape. Fill in the blanks with your own words.

1. **call** it **off**
2. **call** it quits
3. **call** the shots
4. **call** it a day
5. **walk** on air

6. **all talk**
7. **walk all** over
8. It's **all wrong.**
9. It's a **lost cause.**
10. **fought off** an **awful cough**

11. How much does **coffee cost**?
    Coffee costs _____ .
12. What is the **reward for** the **lost dog**?
    The **reward for** the **lost dog** is _____ .
13. Have you had that **awful cough for long**?
    I've had an **awful cough for** _____ .
14. Is **Paul's** hair **long or short**?
    Paul's hair is _____ .
15. Did you make a **long** distance **call** to **Boston or Baltimore**?
    I made a **long** distance **call** to _____ .

78   [ɔ] as in ALL

Listen carefully to your teacher or the tape as five pairs of sentences are presented. **ONE** sentence of each pair will contain a word pronounced with the vowel [ɔ]. Circle the number of the sentence with the [ɔ] word.

EXAMPLE: The instructor says: It's in the **hall.** It's in the **hole.**
              You circle: ①   2

1.   1   2
2.   1   2
3.   1   2
4.   1   2
5.   1   2

SELF-TEST II   (Correct answers may be found in Appendix II on page 175.)

Read the following dialogue aloud. Circle all words that should be pronounced with the vowel [ɔ]. **This self-test is not on the tape.**

. . . .

AUDREY: Hi, Paula. Did you hear the awful news? Maude called off her wedding to Claude!

PAULA: Why, Audrey? I thought they were getting married in August.

AUDREY: Maude kept stalling and decided Claude was the wrong man.

PAULA: Poor Claude. He must be a lost soul.

AUDREY: Oh no. He's abroad in Austria having a ball!

PAULA: I almost forgot. What about the long tablecloth we bought them?

AUDREY: I already brought it back. The cost of the cloth will cover the cost of our lunch today.

PAULA: Audrey, you're always so thoughtful!

. . . .

After checking your answers in Appendix II, practice reading the dialogue again. Remember to protrude your lips and drop your jaw when saying [ɔ].

Listen carefully as your teacher or the instructor on the tape presents ten sentences. Some words that should be pronounced with [ɔ] will be said INCORRECTLY. Circle **"C"** for **CORRECT** or **"I"** for **INCORRECT** to indicate whether the [ɔ] word in each sentence is pronounced properly.

Sentence #	Response		
EXAMPLE:	Ⓒ	I	(She played with the **small** child.)
EXAMPLE:	C	Ⓘ	(Please **sew** the piece of wood.)
1.	C	I	
2.	C	I	
3.	C	I	
4.	C	I	
5.	C	I	
6.	C	I	
7.	C	I	
8.	C	I	
9.	C	I	
10.	C	I	

FOR AN ENCORE ....

Conversation

On the different occasions when you're in a store, ask the commonly heard question, *"How much does it **cost**?"* Whenever you discuss the subject of spending, be sure to use the word *"**cost**"* correctly.

PROTRUDE YOUR LIPS AND DROP YOUR JAW!!!

⟨⟨⟨ *PRACTICE* [ɔ] *OFTEN* ⟩⟩⟩

****

REVIEW OF [ʌ] [oʊ] [ɔ] AND [a]

****

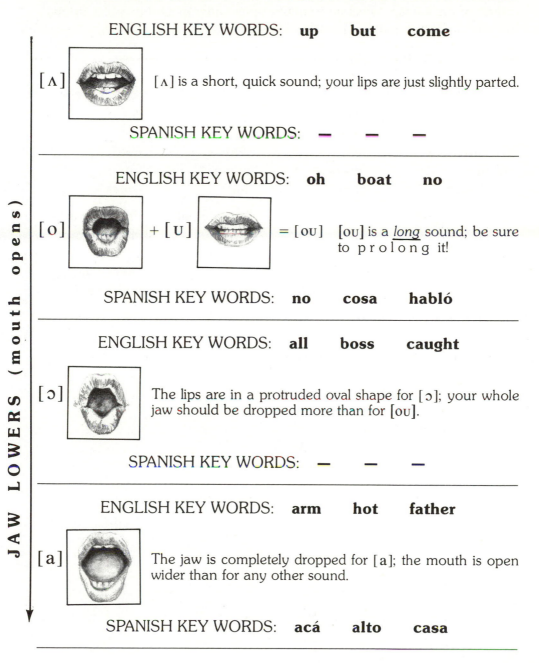

ENGLISH KEY WORDS: **up**   **but**   **come**

[ʌ]   [ʌ] is a short, quick sound; your lips are just slightly parted.

SPANISH KEY WORDS: —   —   —

ENGLISH KEY WORDS: **oh**   **boat**   **no**

[o]   +   [ʊ]   =   [oʊ]   [oʊ] is a *long* sound; be sure to p r o l o n g it!

SPANISH KEY WORDS: **no**   **cosa**   **habló**

ENGLISH KEY WORDS: **all**   **boss**   **caught**

[ɔ]   The lips are in a protruded oval shape for [ɔ]; your whole jaw should be dropped more than for [oʊ].

SPANISH KEY WORDS: —   —   —

ENGLISH KEY WORDS: **arm**   **hot**   **father**

[a]   The jaw is completely dropped for [a]; the mouth is open wider than for any other sound.

SPANISH KEY WORDS: **acá**   **alto**   **casa**

JAW LOWERS (mouth opens)

REVIEW EXERCISE

Repeat the rows of words and sentences accurately after your teacher or the instructor on the tape. Feel your mouth open wider as you progress through the pronunciation of the [ʌ] [ou] [ɔ] and [a] words.

MOUTH OPENS WIDER ──────────────➤

[ʌ]	[ou]	[ɔ]	[a]
1. cut	coat	caught	cot
2. nut	note	naught	not
3. mud	mode	Maude	mod
4. fund	phoned	fawned*	fond
5. Chuck	choke	chalk	chock†
6. The dog bucks.		The dog balks.	The dog barks.
7. Here's a nut.	Here's a note.		Here's a knot.
8. It's in the hull.	It's in the hole.	It's in the hall.	
9. Don't suck it.	Don't soak it.		Don't sock it.
10.	Was it sewed?	Was it sawed?	Was it sod?

11. Don was done at dawn.
    [a]   [ʌ]   [ɔ]

12. Maude mowed the lawn in the mud.
    [ɔ]   [ou]   [ʌ]

13. Bud bought a boat.
    [ʌ]   [ɔ]   [ou]

14. She caught her coat on the cot.
       [ɔ]   [ou]   [a]

15. The caller's collar is a nice color.
    [ɔ]   [a]   [ʌ]

*fawn = lisonjear
†chock = calza; hasta el tope

Your teacher or the instructor on the tape will present the following sentences using **ONE** of the words in parentheses. Listen carefully and circle the word (and vowel) used.

EXAMPLE: The (bald   bold) man is here.
                     [ɔ]   [ou]

1.   His (top   taupe) coat is big.
          [a]   [ou]

2.   The (ball   bowl) fell.
          [ɔ]   [ou]

3.   That (stock   stalk) is still growing.
           [a]   [ɔ]

4.   The (cost   coast) is endless.
          [ɔ]   [ou]

5.   My (luck   lock) is good.
          [ʌ]   [a]

6.   The (lunch   launch) is at three.
           [ʌ]   [ɔ]

7.   She (mops   mopes) at home.
           [a]   [ou]

8.   The (caller   collar) is old.
           [ɔ]   [a]

9.   They (walk   woke) at nine.
            [ɔ]   [ou]

10. The (note   nut) was lost.
           [ou]   [ʌ]

Now that you have completed the review test, read each of the sentences twice. Carefully pronounce the first word in parentheses in the first reading and the contrast word in the second reading.

REVIEW TEST II

(Correct answers may be found in Appendix II on page 176.)

Read the following sentences aloud. In the brackets above each italicized word, write the number of the phonetic symbol representing the sound of the boldface letter(s). **This review test is not on the tape.**

Pronunciation Key: 1 = [ʌ] as in **BUT**   3 = [ɔ] as in **ALL**
                          2 = [ou] as in **NO**   4 = [a] as in **HOT**

EXAMPLE:
    [1]   [2]   [4]
    Chuck choked on the *chopped* beef.

1.
    [ ]   [ ]   [ ]
    Does your *father* like to *doze?*

2.
    [ ] [ ]   [ ]
    A *rolling stone* gathers no *moss.*

3.
    [ ]   [ ] [ ]
    Paul sang the *song* as a *solo.*

4.
    [ ]   [ ] [ ]
    Calm down and *come home.*

5.
    [ ] [ ] [ ]   [ ]
    The *dog dug* a *hole* in the *lawn.*

After checking your answers in Appendix II, practice reading the sentences again.

REVIEW TEST III (Correct answers may be found in Appendix II on page 176.)

Listen carefully to your teacher or the tape as ten groups of three words each are presented. Circle the phonetic symbol that identifies the sound each group of words has in common.

Pronunciation Key: [ʌ] as in *BUT*   [ɔ] as in *ALL*
                                  [oʊ] as in *NO*   [a] as in *HOT*

Group #	Correct Phonetic Symbol						
EXAMPLE :	[ʌ]	[oʊ]	(ɔ)	[a]	(call	story	fought)
EXAMPLE :	[ʌ]	(oʊ)	[ɔ]	[a]	(joke	own	shows)
1.	[ʌ]	[oʊ]	[ɔ]	[a]			
2.	[ʌ]	[oʊ]	[ɔ]	[a]			
3.	[ʌ]	[oʊ]	[ɔ]	[a]			
4.	[ʌ]	[oʊ]	[ɔ]	[a]			
5.	[ʌ]	[oʊ]	[ɔ]	[a]			
6.	[ʌ]	[oʊ]	[ɔ]	[a]			
7.	[ʌ]	[oʊ]	[ɔ]	[a]			
8.	[ʌ]	[oʊ]	[ɔ]	[a]			
9.	[ʌ]	[oʊ]	[ɔ]	[a]			
10.	[ʌ]	[oʊ]	[ɔ]	[a]			

 **REVIEW TEST IV** (Correct answers may be found in Appendix II on page 176.)

Repeat the limericks on the following page, line by line, after your teacher or the instructor on the tape. In the brackets above each italicized word, write the phonetic symbol that represents the sound of the boldface letter(s).

                        [ʌ]   [ʌ]
                A Man *From Kentucky*

                    [ ]   [ ]
        A man from *Kentucky* named *Bud*

        [ ] [ ] [ ]   [ ]
    Had a *lucky young son* named *Jud*

                        [ ]
        When he bet on a *horse*

                [ ]   [ ]
        It never *lost*, of *course*

        [ ]   [ ]   [ ]
    But *one* day it got *stuck* in the *mud*!

....

    [ ] [ ]   [ ]   [ ]
    Tom's father was a *farmer* named *Bob*

        [ ]   [ ] [ ]
    Who *got* very confused *on* the *job*

                [ ]
        Among his misdeeds

                [ ]
        Was mixing *some* seeds

    [ ]   [ ]   [ ]
    His *squash* tasted like *corn* on the *cob*!

....

        [ ]   [ ]   [ ]
    When *Moe* is *home* all *alone*

            [ ]   [ ]
    He just *won't* answer the *phone*

                [ ]   [ ]
        It rings *all* day *long*

                [ ]   [ ]
        From *morning* till *dawn*

        [ ]   [ ]   [ ]
    It's no *wonder* that *Moe* is *unknown*!

....

                    LIMERICKS by P. W. Dale

```
************************************************
```

[ɝ] as in *URN* *FIRST* and *SERVE*

⟨DICTIONARY MARK: ûr⟩

AND

[ɚ] as in *FATHER* and *ACTOR*

⟨DICTIONARY MARK: ər⟩

```
************************************************
```

PRONOUNCING [ɝ]

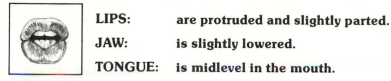

LIPS: are protruded and slightly parted.

JAW: is slightly lowered.

TONGUE: is midlevel in the mouth.

[ɝ] is a sound that occurs only in stressed syllables of words.

POSSIBLE PRONUNCIATION PROBLEMS
FOR THE SPANISH SPEAKER

The vowel [ɝ] does not exist in Spanish. However, Spanish speakers generally have no difficulty producing it. Just remember that [ɝ] always receives strong emphasis and is found only in stressed syllables and words. It is produced with slightly protruded lips and tense tongue muscles. ***Be SURE to practice and you'll be CERTAIN to LEARN* [ɝ]*!!!***

EXERCISE A

The following words should be pronounced with [ɝ]. Repeat them carefully after your teacher or the instructor on the tape.

[ɝ] **At the Beginning**	[ɝ] **In the Middle**	[ɝ] **At the End**
urn	turn	fur
herb	word	blur
earn	verb	stir
earth	third	occur
early	curve	prefer
urgent	learn	
earnest	circus	
	Thursday	

[ɝ] **spelled:**

"ir"	**"ur"**	**"er"**
bird	hurt	fern
girl	curl	term
firm	curb	stern
third	purple	German
circle	turkey	servant

Less frequent spelling patterns for [ɝ] consist of the letters "ear", "our", and "or".

EXAMPLES: h**ear**d   j**our**ney   w**or**k

EXERCISE B

Read the following phrases and sentences aloud. The boldface words should be pronounced with [ɝ]. **This exercise is not on the tape.**

1. **turn** it off
2. **heard** the **words**
3. slow as a **turtle**
4. **first** things **first**
5. the **worst** is yet to come

6. **Herb** left **work early** on **Thursday.**
7. The **early bird** catches the **worm.**
8. The **girl** saw the **circus first.**
9. The **servant served dessert.**
10. **Irma** had **her thirty-third birthday.**

SELF-TEST I   (Correct answers may be found in Appendix II on page 177.)

The boldface words in the following sentences should be pronounced with [ɝ]. Read them aloud; fill in the blanks by selecting the correct word from the list below. **This self-test is not on the tape.**

purse	desserts
perfume	work
curly	turkey
church	verbs
bird	skirt

1. The *girl* wore a *purple* _____ .
2. The *Germans* bake good _____ .
3. At Thanksgiving we *serve* _____ .
4. People *worship* in a _____ .
5. I *heard* the *chirping* of the _____ .
6. Another *word* for handbag is _____ .
7. A *permanent* makes your hair _____ .
8. I *prefer* the scent of that _____ .
9. You should *learn* your nouns and _____ .
10. A *person* collects unemployment when he is out of _____ .

. . . .

PRONOUNCING [ɚ]

It is difficult to hear the difference between [ɚ] and [ɝ] when these sounds are produced in isolation. However, [ɚ] is produced with much less force and occurs only in unstressed syllables of words.

POSSIBLE PRONUNCIATION PROBLEMS FOR THE SPANISH SPEAKER

[ɚ] does not exist in Spanish. The position of the lips and jaw is the same for [ɝ], but unlike the case with [ɝ], the tongue muscles are completely relaxed. [ɚ] never receives strong emphasis and is found only in unstressed syllables of words.

 EXERCISE A

The following words should be pronounced with [ɚ]. Repeat them carefully after your teacher or the instructor on the tape.* Be sure to emphasize [ɚ] less than the other vowels in the words.

[ɚ] **In the Middle**	[ɚ] **At the End**
Saturday	baker
liberty	butter
perhaps	mirror
surprise	mother
afternoon	sooner
butterfly	teacher
flowerpot	deliver
understood	weather

[ɚ] spelled:

"ar"	"er"	"or"	"ure"
sugar	after	color	nature
dollar	paper	actor	picture
collar	father	flavor	feature
regular	farmer	doctor	failure
grammar	silver	razor	measure

*The vowel [ɚ] does not occur at the beginning of words in English.

EXERCISE B

Read the following phrases and sentences aloud. The boldface words should be pronounced with the [ɚ] sound. (Remember, the syllables with [ɚ] are unstressed and should receive much less force than the rest of the word.) **This exercise is not on the tape.**

1. **soon**er or **lat**er
2. **meas**ure the **sug**ar
3. **bett**er late than **never**
4. **consid**er the **off**er
5. **wat**er the **flow**ers

6. The **act**or was **bett**er than **ever**.
7. Was the **afternoon paper delivered**?
8. The **raz**or is **sharp**er than the **sciss**ors.
9. **Summ**er is **warm**er than **wint**er.
10. The **theat**er showed a **wonderful pict**ure.

SELF-TEST I (Correct answers may be found in Appendix II on page 177.)

Read the following words aloud. Circle all the words that are pronounced with [ɚ]. **This self-test is not on the tape.**

(acre)	enter	curtain	dirty
return	third	backward	inform
supper	nurse	soldier	pleasure
purple	silver	weather	Saturday
shirt	mirror	percent	tailor

✳✳
REVIEW OF [ɝ] AND [ɚ]
✳✳

ORAL EXERCISE A

The following words contain both the [ɝ] and [ɚ] sounds. Read them aloud carefully. Be sure to produce the first syllable of each word with much more stress than the second syllable. **This exercise is not on the tape.**

múrder	fírmer	Hérbert
cúrler	sérver	fúrniture
súrfer	búrner	mérger

ORAL EXERCISE B

Read the following phrases and sentences aloud. Be sure to stress the [ɝ] sound and unstress the [ɚ] sound. **This exercise is not on the tape.**

1. silver urn
   [ɚ][ɝ]
2. dangerous curve
   [ɚ]   [ɝ]
3. sermon in church
   [ɝ]   [ɝ]
4. regular exercise
   [ɚ] [ɚ]
5. grammar teacher
   [ɚ]   [ɚ]

6. The grammar teacher worked on verbs.
   [ɚ]   [ɚ] [ɝ]   [ɝ]
7. One good turn deserves another.
   [ɝ]   [ɝ]   [ɚ]
8. Birds of a feather flock together.
   [ɝ]   [ɚ]   [ɚ]
9. Actors perform better after rehearsing.
   [ɚ] [ɚ]   [ɚ] [ɚ]   [ɝ]
10. Mother burned the turkey.
    [ɚ] [ɝ]   [ɝ]

SELF-TEST I   (Correct answers may be found in Appendix II on page 178.)

Each of the following words is pronounced with either the [ɝ] **OR** [ɚ] sound. Circle the phonetic symbol that represents the correct sound. **This self-test is not on the tape.**

EXAMPLE: water   [ɝ]   ([ɚ])

1. learn	[ɝ]	[ɚ]	6. deliver	[ɝ]	[ɚ]
2. sugar	[ɝ]	[ɚ]	7. circus	[ɝ]	[ɚ]
3. picture	[ɝ]	[ɚ]	8. world	[ɝ]	[ɚ]
4. thirsty	[ɝ]	[ɚ]	9. purse	[ɝ]	[ɚ]
5. certain	[ɝ]	[ɚ]	10. urgent	[ɝ]	[ɚ]

SELF-TEST II   (Correct answers may be found in Appendix II on page 178.)

Read the following paragraph about **Pearls** aloud. UNDERLINE all words pronounced with [ɝ] and CIRCLE all words with [ɚ]. **This self-test is not on the tape.**

. . . .

PEARLS

   The **pearl** is one of the most (treasured) gems. Pearls are formed inside the shells of oysters. The largest pearl fisheries are in Asia. Cultured pearls were developed by the Chinese in the twentieth century. They are larger than nature's pearls. A perfect pearl that is round and has great luster is worth a lot of money. Perhaps a "diamond is a girl's best friend," but pearls will always win a woman's favor!

. . . .

FOR AN ENCORE . . . .

Conversation

Make a list of all the occupations you can think of that are pronounced with [ɚ] (i.e., doctor, dancer, banker, etc.). Begin a discussion with a friend about the many different professions and kinds of **work** people do. Every time you use someone's title be sure to pronounce all [ɝ] and [ɚ] words correctly (i.e., **"Mister Rogers is a wonderful teacher"** or "I saw my **lawyer yesterday.**")

```
*************************************************
```

[ə] as in *A UPON* and *SODA*

⟨DICTIONARY MARK: ə⟩

```
*************************************************
```

PRONOUNCING [ə]

[ə] is the sound that results when ANY vowel in English is unstressed in a word. The vowels in all unaccented syllables almost always sound like [ə]. Any letters or combination of letters can represent the schwa [ə].

The schwa vowel is a VERY short, quick sound. Your lips should be completely relaxed and barely move during its production.

POSSIBLE PRONUNCIATION PROBLEMS
FOR THE SPANISH SPEAKER

In Spanish, all vowels are pronounced clearly and distinctly, even in unaccented syllables of words. The schwa [ə] does not exist. In English, unstressed vowels should receive much less force than unstressed vowels do in Spanish. In order to sound like a native English speaker, you must obscure any vowels that are **NOT** in accented syllables of words. Vowel reduction to [ə] is not sloppy speech. It is an important feature of spoken English.

 **EXERCISE A**

Repeat the following words after your teacher or the instructor on the tape. Notice how the syllable with the [ə] vowel receives LESS stress than the other syllables in the word.

[ə] **In the First Syllable**	[ə] **In the Middle**	[ə] **In the Final Syllable**
ago	agony	soda
away	holiday	sofa
along	company	zebra
amaze	buffalo	reason
upon	relative	famous
contain	photograph	lemon
asleep		cousin
suppose		circus
balloon		

[ə] **spelled:**

"a"	"e"	"i"	"o"	"u"
arrive	oven	liquid	occur	upon
ashamed	open	humid	obtain	suppose
asleep	cement	capital	lemon	circus
away	jacket	typical	lesson	column
signal	darkness		contain	

Other spellings of words containing [ə] include "eo", "ou", "iou", and "ai".

EXAMPLES: pig*eo*n   fam*ou*s   delic*iou*s   nat*io*n   cert*ai*n

> **NOTE:** The schwa [ə] can occur more than once and be represented by different letters in the same word.
>
> EXAMPLES: pres*i*d*e*nt   *e*l*e*ph*a*nt   acc*i*d*e*nt

EXERCISE B

Read the following common phrases and sentences aloud. Be sure to pronounce the syllable with [ə] with LESS force than the other syllables. **This exercise is not on the tape.**

1. How are you today?
2. See you tonight.
3. See you tomorrow.
4. Don't complain.
5. I suppose so.
6. I suppose its possible.
7. Consider my complaint.
8. Complete today's lesson.
9. Don't complain about the problem.
10. My cousin will arrive at seven.

 **SELF-TEST I**   (Correct answers may be found in Appendix II on page 178.)

Repeat the following words after your teacher or the instructor on the tape. Circle the schwa vowel [ə] in the ONE unstressed syllable in each word.

EXAMPLES: a. tel(e)graph
            b. rabb(i)t

1. alphabet
2. utilize
3. depending
4. photograph
5. papa

6. prevent
7. imitate
8. breakfast
9. control
10. alarm

SELF-TEST II

(Correct answers may be found in Appendix II on page 178.)

Read each four-word series aloud. Circle the **ONE** word in each group of four that does **NOT** contain [ə]. **This self-test is not on the tape.**

EXAMPLE: (slipper)   soda   finally   agree

1.	about	oven	create	olive
2.	minute	second	seven	leaving
3.	attic	attend	allow	annoy
4.	something	support	supply	suppose
5.	combine	complete	camper	compare
6.	Canada	Georgia	Tennessee	Wyoming
7.	lavender	maroon	yellow	orange
8.	strawberry	banana	vanilla	chocolate
9.	lettuce	tomato	carrot	cucumber
10.	giraffe	zebra	monkey	camel

SELF-TEST III

(Correct answers may be found in Appendix II on page 179.)

Read the following words aloud. Each word contains TWO unstressed syllables. Circle the schwa [ə] vowels in **BOTH** unstressed syllables of each word. **This self-test is not on the tape.**

EXAMPLES: a. m a g i c a l
            b. e l e p h a n t

1. f a v o r i t e
2. p r i n c i p a l
3. a s s i s t a n c e
4. m e d i c a l
5. a t t e n d a n c e

6. e v i d e n c e
7. o f f e n d e d
8. d i p l o m a
9. a p a r t m e n t
10. C a n a d a

[ə] as in A   **97**

FOR AN ENCORE ···

Reading

Open a book you are reading to any page. Choose any five lines on the page and circle all words pronounced with [ə]. Read the five lines aloud. Be sure to **unstress** the [ə] vowel in the circled words. Repeat any words you have difficulty with.

You're really making progress. KEEP UP THE GREAT WORK! Why don't you take a coffee break at this point? YOU DESERVE IT!

```
*********************************************
```

[aʊ] as in *OUT HOUSE* and *COW*
⟨DICTIONARY MARK: ou⟩

```
*********************************************
```

PRONOUNCING [aʊ]

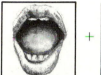 +

LIPS: glide from an open position.

JAW: rises with the tongue and closes.

TONGUE: glides from low to high near the roof of the mouth.

[aʊ] is a diphthong. It begins with [a] and ends with [ʊ]. [aʊ] is pronounced the same way as the Spanish letters "au".

SPANISH KEY WORDS WITH [aʊ]

Spanish words with this sound are spelled with "au".

KEY WORDS: *auto*   *aunque*   *pausa*   *causa*

POSSIBLE PRONUNCIATION PROBLEMS FOR THE SPANISH SPEAKER

[aʊ] is a familiar Spanish sound and shouldn't present any difficulty for you in English. Just remember that [aʊ] is always represented by the letter "o" followed by "u", "w", or "ugh".

EXAMPLES: **ou**t   c**ow**   pl**ough**

You already PRONOUNCE [aʊ] in Spanish. Think of the Spanish key words PAUSA and AUTO; you won't have DOUBTS ABOUT the SOUND [aʊ]!!!

EXERCISE A

The following words should all be pronounced with [aʊ]. Repeat them carefully after your teacher or the instructor on the tape.

[aʊ] **At the Beginning**	[aʊ] **In the Middle**	[aʊ] **At the End**
owl	loud	cow
our	down	how
out	brown	now
hour	crowd	allow
ounce	mouse	plough
outfit	vowel	
ourselves	flower	
	mountain	
	pronounce	

[aʊ] **spelled:**

"ou"	"ow"
foul	town
sour	crown
cloud	power
thousand	eyebrow
announce	somehow

A less frequent spelling pattern for [aʊ] consists of the letters "ough."

EXAMPLES: b**ough**   dr**ough**t   pl**ough**

EXERCISE B

Read the following phrases and sentences aloud. The boldface words should be pronounced with the diphthong [aʊ]. (Remember [aʊ] is just like the letters "au" in *auto* or *causa*.) **This exercise is not on the tape.**

1. **How** are you?
2. **How about** it?
3. **Count** me **out**!
4. I **doubt** it!
5. **hour** after **hour**
6. **around** the **house**

7. **vowel sounds**
   Pronounce the **vowel sounds**.
8. **shout out loud**
   Don't **shout out loud** in the **house**.
9. **out** of **bounds***
   The ball **bounced out** of **bounds**.
10. is **proud**
    Howard is **proud** of his **flowers**.

SELF-TEST I   (Correct answers may be found in Appendix II on page 179.)

Read each series of four words out loud. Circle the **ONE** word in each group of four that is **NOT** pronounced with [aʊ]. **This self-test is not on the tape.**

EXAMPLE:	bounce	round	found	would
1.	brown	down	flow	frown
2.	foul	group	shout	loud
3.	know	how	now	cow
4.	sour	hour	tour	our
5.	could	count	crown	crowd
6.	thought	plough	drought†	thousand
7.	ounce	out	own	ouch
8.	flounder	flood	flour	pounce
9.	allow	about	power	arose
10.	noun	consonant	vowel	sound

*out of bounds = fuera de la cancha
†drought = sequía

SELF-TEST II   (Correct answers may be found in Appendix II on page 179.)

Read the following dialogue aloud. Circle all words that should be pronounced with the diphthong [au]. **This self-test is not on the tape.**

. . . .

MR. BROWN: You look (out) of sorts. (How) come?

MRS. BROWN: I'm tired out. Didn't you hear the loud noise outside all night?

MR. BROWN: I didn't hear a sound. I was "out like a light"!

MRS. BROWN: Our neighbors had a big crowd; they were shouting and howling!

MR. BROWN: Why didn't you tell them to stop clowning around?

MRS. BROWN: I didn't want to sound like a grouch.

MR. BROWN: Next time I'll go out. I'm not afraid to open my mouth!

MRS. BROWN: I knew I could count on you. Here comes our noisy neighbor Mr. Crowley, right now.

MR. BROWN: That 300-pound "powerhouse"! Sorry dear, I have to go downtown, NOW!!

MRS. BROWN: Come back, you coward!!!

. . . .

After checking your answers in Appendix II, practice reading the dialogue again. Remember to pronounce [au] the same way as in Spanish!

FOR AN ENCORE . . . .

Conversation

Start a conversation using as many **"HOW"** questions as you can think of. (**How** do you do? **How** are you? **How's** the weather **out**side? etc.) Be sure to pronounce [au] the same way as in the Spanish word *"auto."*

PRACTICE [au] OUT LOUD ***

⟨⟨⟨ *YOU WON'T HAVE DOUBTS ABOUT THE SOUND* [au] ⟩⟩⟩

```
*****************************************************
```

[aɪ] as in *I MY* and *PIE*
⟨DICTIONARY MARK: ī⟩

```
*****************************************************
```

PRONOUNCING [aɪ]

 +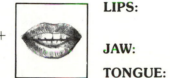

LIPS: glide from an open to a slightly parted position.

JAW: rises with the tongue and closes.

TONGUE: glides from low to high near the roof of the mouth.

[aɪ] is a diphthong. It begins with [a] and ends with [ɪ]. [aɪ] is pronounced the same way as the Spanish letters "ai" or "ay".

SPANISH KEY WORDS WITH [aɪ]

Spanish words with this sound are spelled with "ay" or "ai".

KEY WORDS: *hay   aire   paisaje   bailar*

POSSIBLE PRONUNCIATION PROBLEMS FOR THE SPANISH SPEAKER

The diphthong [aɪ] should be quite easy for you to pronounce in English. Just be careful of irregular spelling patterns. Remember that [aɪ] is frequently represented by the letters "i" or "y".

EXAMPLES: **i**ce   m**y**

When practicing [aɪ], keep the Spanish key words HAY and AIRE in MIND; your pronunciation of [aɪ] will be QUITE FINE!!!

EXERCISE A

The following words should all be pronounced with [aɪ]. Carefully repeat them after your teacher or the instructor on the tape.

[aɪ] **At the Beginning**	[aɪ] **In the Middle**	[aɪ] **At the End**
eye	bite	by
ice	five	cry
I'm	life	dry
I've	mind	die
item	sign	tie
aisle	fight	lie
island	rhyme	rye
	while	deny
	light	

[aɪ] **spelled:**

"i"	"y"	"ie"	"igh"
I	my	die	high
ice	fly	pie	sight
fire	why	tie	night
bite	type	cries	delight
nice	style	fried	frighten

> **HINTS:**
> a. The letter "i" followed by "gh" "ld" or "nd" is usually pronounced [aɪ].
>
>   EXAMPLES: s**igh**t w**ild** f**ind**
>
> b. When "i" is in a syllable ending in silent "e," the letter "i" is pronounced [aɪ] (the same name as the alphabet letter "I"!!!).
>
>   EXAMPLES: b**i**te f**i**ne ref**i**nement conf**i**ne

EXERCISE B

Read the following phrases and sentences aloud. The boldface words should be pronounced with the diphthong [aɪ]. (Think of the Spanish Key Word *hay* and your pronunciation will be right!) **This exercise is not on the tape.**

1. **Hi**!
2. **Nice** to meet you.
3. **I'm fine.**

4. What **time** is it?
5. **Nice try**!
6. **Rise** and **shine**!

7. **nine** to **five**
   The store is open from **nine** to **five**.
8. the **price** is **right**
   I'll buy the **item** if the **price** is **right**.
9. **by tonight**
   I'll try to **type** it **by tonight**.
10. **driver's license**
    My driver's license expires in **July**.

SELF-TEST I (Correct answers may be found in Appendix II on page 180.)

Read each series of four words out loud. Circle the **ONE** word in each group of four that is **NOT** pronounced with [aɪ]. **This self-test is not on the tape.**

EXAMPLE:	pie	line	(rich)	rice
1.	price	crime	pity	pile
2.	mind	kind	spinning	finding
3.	sign	high	fright	freight
4.	list	cite	aisle	cried
5.	gyp	bye	cry	reply
6.	niece	nice	knife	night
7.	style	failed	filed	fire
8.	pretty	try	resign	goodbye
9.	ice cream	eye	aim	aisle
10.	flight	fine	duty	dying

SELF-TEST II   (Correct answers may be found in Appendix II on page 180.)

Read the following dialogue aloud. Circle all words that should be pronounced with the diphthong [aɪ]. **This self-test is not on the tape.**

. . . .

MIKE: (Hi), (Myra)! It's (nice) to see you.
MYRA: Likewise,* Mike. How are you?
MIKE: I'm tired. I just came in on a night flight from Ireland.
MYRA: What time did your flight arrive?
MIKE: I arrived at five forty-five in the morning.
MYRA: I'm surprised the airlines have a late night flight.
MIKE: If you don't mind, Myra, I think I'll go home and rest for a while. I'm really "wiped out"!†
MYRA: It's quite all right. Goodbye, Mike!

. . . .

After checking your answers in Appendix II, practice reading the dialogue again. Remember to pronounce [aɪ] the same way as in Spanish!

FOR AN ENCORE . . . .

Reading

Before going to a movie, read the movie guide in your newspaper. Underline all the [aɪ] words in the titles of the movies being advertised. Practice reading the titles out loud.

KEEP TRYING!!!

⟨⟨⟨ *YOUR* [a̲ɪ] *WILL BE QUI̲TE FI̲NE* ⟩⟩⟩

*likewise = igualmente

†I'm wiped out = estoy agotado

106   [aɪ] as in I

****

[ɔɪ] as in *OIL NOISE* and *BOY*

⟨DICTIONARY MARK: oi⟩

****

PRONOUNCING [ɔɪ]

 +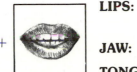

LIPS: glide from a tense oval shape to a relaxed, slightly parted position.

JAW: rises with the tongue and closes.

TONGUE: glides from a low position to high near the roof of the mouth.

[ɔɪ] is a diphthong. It begins with [ɔ] and ends with [ɪ]. [ɔɪ] **is pronounced the same way as the Spanish letters "oy" or "oi".**

SPANISH KEY WORDS WITH [ɔɪ]

Spanish words with this sound are spelled with "oy" or "oi".

KEY WORDS: *hoy*   *soy*   *sois*   *oiga*

POSSIBLE PRONUNCIATION PROBLEMS FOR THE SPANISH SPEAKER

You shouldn't have ANY problem at all with the diphthong [ɔɪ]. Its pronunciation will be simple for you. Just as in Spanish, English words with this diphthong are spelled with "oy" or "oi". There are virtually no exceptions to this rule!

When practicing the exercises, remember that the letters "oy" and "oi" sound the same as they do in Spanish. **Think of the Spanish key word S<u>O</u>Y and you'll ENJ<u>OY</u> pronouncing [<u>ɔɪ</u>]!**

The following words should all be pronounced with [ɔɪ]. Repeat them as accurately as possible after your teacher or the instructor on the tape.

[ɔɪ] **At the Beginning**	[ɔɪ] **In the Middle**	[ɔɪ] **At the End**
oil	join	toy
oink	broil	boy
oily	boil	joy
oyster	foil	ploy
ointment	coin	enjoy
	avoid	annoy
	noise	alloy
	poison	decoy
	choice	destroy

EXERCISE B

Repeat the following phrases and questions/answers aloud. The boldface words should all be pronounced with [ɔɪ]. Fill in the blanks with your own words. **This exercise is not on the tape.**

1. girls and **boys**
2. flip a **coin**
3. Don't **annoy** me!
4. **Enjoy** yourself.
5. Lower your **voice**.
6. Do you like **broiled** or **boiled oysters**?
   I like _____ _____ .
7. Do you need **oil** or **foil**?
   I need _____ .
8. Did you buy **choice sirloin** or pork **loin**?
   I bought _____ .
9. Are **noisy** children **annoying** or **enjoyable**?
   Noisy children are _____ .
10. Would you **enjoy** a trip to **Detroit** or **St. Croix**?
    I'd **enjoy** going to _____ !

SELF-TEST I

(Correct answers may be found in Appendix II on page 180.)

Read each four-word series aloud. Circle the **ONE** word in each group that is **NOT** pronounced with [ɔɪ]. **This self-test is not on the tape.**

EXAMPLE: joy   join   enjoy   (jaunt)

1. voice   avoid   void   vows
2. noise   nose   hoist   annoy
3. towel   toy   toil   spoil
4. Detroit   Illinois   St. Croix   New York
5. oil   oily   foil   owl
6. boil   broil   bow   boy
7. poison   pounce   point   appoint
8. poise   Joyce   Joan   soil
9. coil   coal   coy   coin
10. lobster   sirloin   oyster   moist

SELF-TEST II

(Correct answers may be found in Appendix II on page 181.)

Read the following dialogue aloud. Circle all words that should be pronounced with the diphthong [ɔɪ]. **This self-test is not on the tape.**

. . . .

MRS. ROYCE: Hi, Mr. (Lloyd.) Can I help you?
MR. LLOYD: Yes, Mrs. (Royce.) I'd like a (toy) for my son (Floyd.)
MRS. ROYCE: We have quite a choice of toys. What about a firetruck?
MR. LLOYD: That's too noisy. Besides, my boy would destroy it!
MRS. ROYCE: Here's a paint and oil set.
MR. LLOYD: That's messy. His mother will be annoyed if he soils any-
                 thing.
MRS. ROYCE: Let me point out this electric train.
MR. LLOYD: Wow! I never had a toy like that as a boy!
MRS. ROYCE: Your boy will enjoy it. Mr. Lloyd? Please turn off the set. Mr.
                 Lloyd, you can't hear my voice!!
MR. LLOYD: Did you say something, Mrs. Royce? I'm playing with Floyd's
                 new toy!
MRS. ROYCE: I guess he's made his choice. I hope he lets his boy use it
                 once in a while!

. . . .

[ɔɪ] as in OIL   **109**

After checking your answers in Appendix II, practice reading the dialogue again. Be sure to pronounce [ɔɪ] like the Spanish letters "oi" or "oy".

FOR AN ENCORE ....

Conversation

Whenever you must schedule an appointment with someone (your doctor, lawyer, hairdresser, teacher, etc.) use the phrase *"I'd like to make an ap-pointment with _____ ."* Be sure to pronounce [ɔɪ] correctly.

THINK OF THE SPANISH WORD "SOY"!!!

⟨⟨⟨ *YOU'LL ENJOY PRONOUNCING* [ɔɪ] ⟩⟩⟩

REVIEW OF [ə] [aʊ] [aɪ] AND [ɔɪ]

****

ENGLISH KEY WORDS: **a   upon   soda**

[ə]   ([ə] is a short, quick sound; your lips should barely move.)

SPANISH KEY WORDS: —   —   —

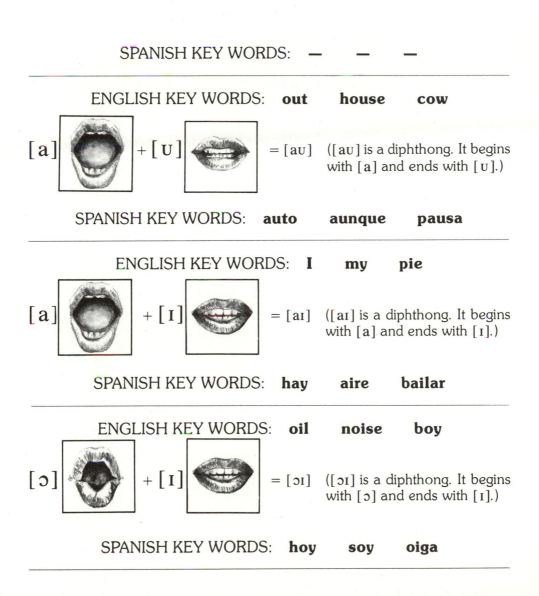

ENGLISH KEY WORDS: **out   house   cow**

[a] + [ʊ] = [aʊ] ([aʊ] is a diphthong. It begins with [a] and ends with [ʊ].)

SPANISH KEY WORDS: **auto   aunque   pausa**

ENGLISH KEY WORDS: **I   my   pie**

[a] + [ɪ] = [aɪ] ([aɪ] is a diphthong. It begins with [a] and ends with [ɪ].)

SPANISH KEY WORDS: **hay   aire   bailar**

ENGLISH KEY WORDS: **oil   noise   boy**

[ɔ] + [ɪ] = [ɔɪ] ([ɔɪ] is a diphthong. It begins with [ɔ] and ends with [ɪ].)

SPANISH KEY WORDS: **hoy   soy   oiga**

REVIEW EXERCISE

Read the following rows of words and sentences aloud as accurately as possible. **This review exercise is not on the tape.**

[aʊ]	[aɪ]	[ɔɪ]
1. bow	buy	boy
2. owl	aisle	oil
3. foul	file	foil
4. vowed	vied	void
5. loud	lied	Lloyd
6. What a bow!	What a buy!	What a boy!
7. It's a foul.	It's a file.	It's a foil.
8. I found the owl.	I found the aisle.	I found the oil.
9. Spell "loud."	Spell "lied."	Spell "Lloyd."
10. The towel was long.	The tile was long.	The toil was long.

11. **I** saw the b**oy** take a b**ow**.
   [aɪ]   [ɔɪ]   [aʊ]

12. Ll**oy**d is not **allow**ed **ou**tside.
   [ɔɪ]   [ə][aʊ] [aʊ]

13. V**io**la v**ow**ed to **avoi**d advice.
   [aɪ] [aʊ]   [ə][ɔɪ]   [aɪ]

14. The plur**al** of m**ou**se is m**i**ce.
       [ə]   [aʊ]   [aɪ]

15. The n**oi**sy cr**ow**d cr**i**ed **alou**d.
       [ɔɪ]   [aʊ] [aɪ] [ə][aʊ]

REVIEW TEST I

(Correct answers may be found in Appendix II on page 181.)

Read the following words aloud. Write each word under the symbol that represents the sound of the boldface letter(s). **This review test is not on the tape.**

j**oi**n	fr**i**ght	rh**y**me	cir**c**us
br**i**ght	s**ou**nd	v**ow**	l**oy**al
fr**ow**n	destr**oy**	v**oy**age	cl**ou**d
alone	wh**i**le	op**e**n	hum**i**d
upon	b**oi**l	g**ui**de	rel**y**
m**ou**th	lem**o**n	m**ou**ntain	n**oi**se

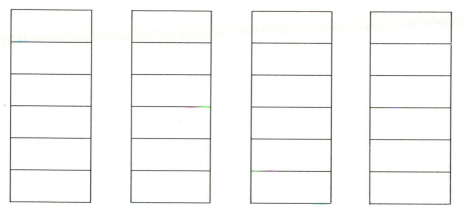

[ə] **as in UPON**	[aʊ] **as in OUT**	[aɪ] **as in I**	[ɔɪ] **as in OIL**

After checking your answers in Appendix II, carefully pronounce all of the above words again.

REVIEW TEST II   <small>(Correct answers may be found in Appendix II on page 181.)</small>

Read aloud the following recipe. On the line above each word write the number of the phonetic symbol that represents the sound of the boldface letters. **This review test is not on the tape.**

Pronunciation Key: 1 = [ə] as in UPON
2 = [aʊ] as in OUT
3 = [aɪ] as in I
4 = [ɔɪ] as in OIL

   3   1

Frīed chick**e**n is līked through**ou**t the Unīted States. H**o**w**e**ver, it is c**o**nsidered a fam**ou**s dish from the S**ou**th. Here is the recipe for you to enj**oy**.

Ingredi**e**nts:

One frȳing chicken (ab**ou**t three or four p**ou**nds)

One cup of fl**ou**r

Eight **ou**nces of **oi**l

Comb**i**ne fl**ou**r with seas**o**nings of your own ch**oi**ce. Roll chicken in flour and coat on all sīdes. Pour **oi**l into large-sīzed frȳing pan. Heat oil until very hot (almost b**oi**ling). Fry three or four pieces at a tīme including breasts, wings and th**i**ghs. Cover tīghtly and cook for ar**ou**nd twenty-fīve minutes. All**ow** chicken to steam. Remove cover and cook for nīne or ten minutes more until pieces are c**o**mpletely br**ow**ned. Take chicken **ou**t of pan and drȳ on paper t**ow**el.

****

GENERAL REVIEW ACTIVITIES

****

The general review activities that follow are designed to assess the skills you have developed. They also serve as more material to help you practice everything you have learned.

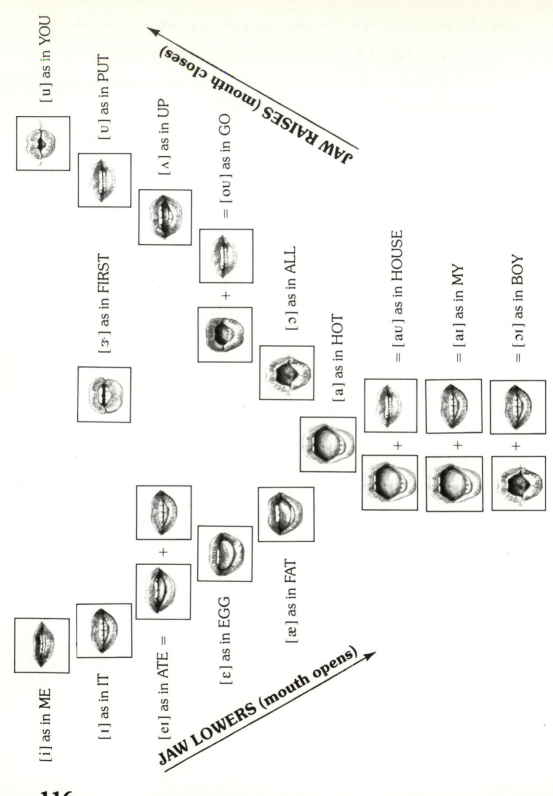

[u] as in YOU

[ʊ] as in PUT

[ʌ] as in UP

= [oʊ] as in GO

JAW RAISES (mouth closes)

[ɝ] as in FIRST

+

[ɔ] as in ALL

[a] as in HOT

= [aʊ] as in HOUSE

= [aɪ] as in MY

= [ɔɪ] as in BOY

+

+

+

[i] as in ME

[ɪ] as in IT

[eɪ] as in ATE =

+

[ɛ] as in EGG

[æ] as in FAT

JAW LOWERS (mouth opens)

116

****

GENERAL REVIEW ACTIVITIES
FOR VOWELS AND DIPHTHONGS

****

GENERAL REVIEW ACTIVITY I

(Correct answers may be found in Appendix II on page 182.)

These practice words are 100 of the most frequently used words in English. Read each word aloud, then write it under the appropriate phonetic symbol. **This review activity is not on the tape.**

1. the	21. you	41. because	61. course	81. person
2. and	22. we	42. light	62. other	82. way
3. of	23. one	43. at	63. from	83. first
4. a	24. an	44. by	64. what	84. my
5. to	25. as	45. man	65. than	85. about
6. in	26. not	46. these	66. two	86. should
7. it	27. if	47. can	67. think	87. great
8. is	28. make	48. so	68. them	88. well
9. that	29. on	49. his	69. school	89. give
10. have	30. there	50. time	70. up	90. day
11. this	31. was	51. out	71. who	91. only
12. be	32. or	52. when	72. their	92. see
13. work	33. all	53. our	73. know	93. then
14. I	34. but	54. some	74. want	94. also
15. are	35. will	55. take	75. her	95. each
16. they	36. would	56. has	76. state	96. may
17. do	37. with	57. thing	77. were	97. too
18. for	38. which	58. very	78. just	98. any
19. he	39. people	59. much	79. been	99. like
20. many	40. more	60. she	80. could	100. most

[i]	[ɪ]	[eɪ]	[ɛ]	[æ]	[a]	[u]
be	in	they	many	and	are	to

[ʊ]	[ʌ]	[ou]	[ɔ]	[ɝ]	[aɪ]	[au]
would	the	so	for	work	I	out

GENERAL REVIEW ACTIVITY II

(Correct answers may be found in Appendix II on page 183.)

Listen carefully to your teacher or the tape as ten groups of three words are presented. Circle the phonetic symbol that identifies the sound each group of words has in common.

EXAMPLE: The instructor says: heat   mean   cheese
                    You circle: [ɛ]   ⓘ   [ɪ]

1.	[ɛ]	[ɪ]	[i]		6.	[u]	[ʊ]	[ʌ]
2.	[ɛ]	[ɪ]	[i]		7.	[aɪ]	[ɔ]	[ou]
3.	[eɪ]	[a]	[æ]		8.	[aɪ]	[ɔ]	[ou]
4.	[eɪ]	[a]	[æ]		9.	[au]	[ɔɪ]	[ɝ]
5.	[u]	[ʊ]	[ʌ]		10.	[au]	[ɔɪ]	[ɝ]

Listen carefully to your teacher or the tape as the following five-word series are presented. UNDERLINE the **ONE** word in each group of five that is pronounced with a vowel different from the other words. CIRCLE the phonetic symbol representing the vowel common to the other four.

EXAMPLES: a. (⟨u⟩) [ou] [ɔ]   true   student   four   group   new
          b. [a] (⟨ɝ⟩) [aɪ]   park   nurse   third   learn   burn

1. [ʌ]	[ou]	[ɔ]	us	country	subject	women	come
2. [ɔ]	[eɪ]	[æ]	play	change	back	made	raise
3. [i]	[ɪ]	[ɛ]	mean	speech	teacher	need	subject
4. [a]	[æ]	[eɪ]	example	back	after	rather	part
5. [æ]	[eɪ]	[ɛ]	help	less	second	number	said
6. [a]	[ou]	[ɔ]	large	job	home	top	college
7. [i]	[ɪ]	[aɪ]	quite	him	picture	into	little
8. [aɪ]	[eɪ]	[au]	might	why	high	life	say
9. [aɪ]	[au]	[ɔɪ]	down	around	how	those	now
10. [ɔ]	[a]	[ou]	before	small	long	old	cost

After checking your answers in Appendix II, carefully pronounce the above words. (These words are among the second 100 most common words in the English language.)

Repeat the following sentences after your teacher or the instructor on the tape. Fill in the blanks with a RHYME word for the one in italics.

EXAMPLE: [ʌ]   I saw the **BUG** running on the **R**UG_____ .

1.   [ɛ]   The kids were **FED** and put to **B**_____ .
2.   [aɪ]   The shining **LIGHT** was very **BR**_____ .
3.   [aʊ]   We heard the crowd **SHOUT** as the batter struck **O**_____ .
4.   [oʊ]   My friend **ROSE** wears pretty **CL**_____ .
5.   [eɪ]   Kate made a **DATE**; don't be **L**_____ .
6.   [a]   After **DARK** the dogs start to **B**_____ .
7.   [u]   It's too **COOL** in the swimming **P**_____ .
8.   [ɔɪ]   Roy gave my **BOY** a brand new **T**_____ .
9.   [ʊ]   Be sure to **LOOK** in the phone **B**_____ .
10.   [æ]   Why does **DAD** look unhappy and **S**_____ ?

GENERAL REVIEW ACTIVITY V

(Correct answers may be found in Appendix II on page 184.)

Read the following poem by Joyce Kilmer aloud. In the brackets provided, write the phonetic symbol that represents the sound of the underlined letter(s). Select the correct phonetic symbol from those to the right. **This review activity is not on the tape.**

[ɪ]   [ɔɪ]
TREES was written by Joyce Kilmer   [ɪ]   [i]   [ɔɪ]

[ ]   [ ] [ ]
I think that I shall never see   [ɪ]   [i]   [ɛ]

[ ]   [ ][ ]
A poem as lovely as a tree   [ʌ]   [i]   [ə]

[ ]   [ ]
A tree whose hungry mouth is prest   [u]   [ou]   [au]

[ ]   [ ]   [ ]
Against the earth's sweet flowing breast;   [ɛ]   [ɝ]   [ɛ]

[ ]   [ ][ ]
A tree that looks at God all day,   [a]   [ɔ]   [u]

[ ]   [ ]   [ ]
And lifts her leafy arms to pray;   [a]   [eɪ]   [ɪ]

[ ]   [ ]
A tree that may in summer wear   [æ]   [ɝ]   [a]

[ ] [ ]
A nest of robins in her hair;   [a]   [eɪ]   [ɛ]

[ ]   [ ]   [ ]
Upon whose bosom snow has lain   [ə]   [eɪ]   [ou]

[ ]   [ ]
Who intimately lives with rain.   [u]   [eɪ]   [ɪ]

[ ]   [ ][ ]
Poems are made by fools like me   [u]   [eɪ]   [aɪ]

[ ]   [ ]
But only God can make a tree.   [i]   [ou]   [a]

After checking your answers in Appendix II, practice reading **"TREES"** again.

INTRODUCING STRESS, RHYTHM, AND INTONATION

Thus far, you have been studying the individual sounds of English. These sounds can be significantly affected by vocal features known as stress, rhythm, and intonation. These *vocal features* help to convey meaning and must be used correctly if you are to be completely understood.

STRESS is the first vocal feature we will deal with. Speakers must stress certain syllables in words; otherwise the words would be misunderstood or sound strange. You are already familiar with this feature in Spanish. It is through **stress** that you can distinguish between *papa* and *papá, seria* and *sería,* or *libro* and *libró.* Stress can also change the meaning of a sentence: *"El HOMBRE me habló"* is different from *"El hombre me HABLÓ."* In English, proper use of stress enables you to clearly understand the difference between such words as **pres**ent *(regalo)* and pre**sent** *(presentar).* "HE won't go" implies a meaning different from *"He won't GO."*

RHYTHM is the second feature we will present. Rhythm is created by the strong stresses or *beats* in a sentence. In Spanish, the rhythm is *syllable-timed.* This means that all vowels in all syllables are pronounced almost equally. Syllables are rarely lost or reduced as they are in English. For example, the three-word phrase *"huevos con jamón"* would never become two words. But, in English, *"ham and eggs"* is squeezed into two words, *"ham'n eggs."*

This reduction results because English has a *stress-timed* rhythm. This means that its rhythm is determined by the number of stresses and not by the number of syllables. English speakers slow down and emphasize heavily stressed words or syllables. They speed up and reduce unstressed ones. For example, the five-word phrase "I will see you tomorrow" may become *"I'll seeya t'morrow."*

INTONATION is the final vocal feature you will learn about. Intonation patterns involve pitch and are responsible for the melody of the language. Speakers frequently depend more on intonation patterns to convey their meaning than on the pronunciation of the individual vowels and consonants. For example, in Spanish you can use the exact words to make a statement or ask a question. If your vocal intonation rises, you are asking the question *¿Habla inglés?* If your voice falls, you are making the statement *Habla inglés.* The same thing occurs in English. The sentence *That's Bill's car* becomes the question *That's Bill's car?* when you raise the pitch of your voice at the end. So—now you can appreciate the common expression, **It's not WHAT you say, it's HOW you say it!**

Although your English grammar might be perfect and you can pronounce individual sounds correctly, you will still have a noticeable foreign accent until you master the **stress, rhythm,** and **intonation** patterns of English.

```
************************************************
```

STRESS WITHIN THE WORD

```
************************************************
```

DEFINITION

Stress refers to the amount of volume that a speaker gives to a particular sound, syllable, or word while saying it. Stressed sounds and syllables are **louder** and longer than unstressed ones. The words *accent, stress,* and *emphasis* are frequently used interchangeably.

STRESS IN ENGLISH

A major characteristic of the English language is the use of strong and weak stress. Every word of more than one syllable has a syllable that is emphasized more than the others. Accented syllables receive more force and are **louder** than unaccented ones. Correct use of stress is essential for achieving proper pronunciation of words.

POSSIBLE PRONUNCIATION PROBLEMS FOR THE SPANISH SPEAKER

The Spanish language has specific rules for accenting words. When there is an exception to the rule, an accent mark is generally written above the stressed syllable. There are **NO** consistent rules in English. Consequently, you may have difficulty when attempting to accent syllables correctly.

1. You may place the stress on the **wrong** syllable.

   EXAMPLES: désert (desierto) would sound like dessért (postre)
   ínvalid (enfermizo) would sound like inválid (nulo)

2. You may stress every vowel in a word equally and forget to reduce vowels in unaccented syllables (refer back to page 94).

   EXAMPLES: tomórrow would sound like tómórrów
   becáuse would sound like bécáuse

As you practice imitating your teacher or the instructor on the tapes, your ability to use proper stress patterns when speaking English will improve. ***BE POSITIVE AND KEEP PRACTICING!***

WORDS STRESSED ON THE FIRST SYLLABLE

I. **The majority of two-syllable words are accented on the FIRST syllable.**

EXAMPLES: Túesday   áwful   éver   bróther   óven   wíndow

II. **Compound nouns are usually accented on the FIRST syllable.**

EXAMPLES: bédroom   aírfield   stóplight   schóolhouse   bóokstore

III. **Numbers that are multiples of ten are accented on the FIRST syllable.**

EXAMPLES: twénty   thírty   fórty   fífty   síxty   séventy

WORDS STRESSED ON THE SECOND SYLLABLE

I. **Reflexive pronouns are usually accented on the SECOND syllable.**

EXAMPLES: mysélf   yoursélf   himsélf   hersélf   oursélves

II. **Compound verbs are usually accented on the SECOND or LAST syllable.**

EXAMPLES: outdóne   outsmárt   outdó   outrún   overloók   overcóme

EXERCISE A

Repeat the following words as accurately as possible after your teacher or the instructor on the tape. Be sure to stress the **first** syllable of the words in Column I and the **second** syllable of the words in Column II.

Stress on the FIRST Syllable	Stress on the SECOND Syllable
ápple	aróund
táble	allów
móther	invíte
téacher	compléte
wínter	suppórt
páper	beliéve
báseball	mysélf
bréakfast	outrún
síxty	behínd
eíghty	overdúe

EXERCISE B

The following three-syllable words have a variety of stress patterns. Repeat them as accurately as possible after your teacher or the instructor on the tape. **Remember** to EMPHASIZE the stressed syllable.

Primary Stress on the FIRST SYLLABLE	Primary Stress on the SECOND SYLLABLE	Primary Stress on the THIRD SYLLABLE
áccident	accéptance	afternóon
stráwberry	vanílla	absolúte
séventy	exámine	seventéen
yésterday	tomórrow	recomménd
président	políceman	guaranteé
sálary	emplóyer	employeé
pérsonal	repáirman	personnél
tránslating	translátion	gasolíne
élephant	gorílla	kangaroó
Fébruary	Decémber	overloók

STRESS IN NOUN/VERB PAIRS

There are many nouns and verbs that are the same in the written form. We can distinguish between these word pairs in their spoken form through the use of stress. In these pairs, the noun will always be stressed on the first syllable, the verb on the second syllable.

EXERCISE C

Repeat the following noun/verb pairs after your teacher or instructor on the tape. Remember to stress the **noun** on the FIRST syllable and the **verb** on the SECOND.

Nouns		**Verbs**	
cónflict	(conflicto)	conflíct	(oponerse)
cónduct	(conducta)	condúct	(conducir, portarse)
cóntent	(contenido)	contént	(satisfacer)
désert	(desierto)	desért	(abandonar)
dígest	(sumario)	digést	(digerir)
cóntest	(concurso)	contést	(contender)
pérmit	(permiso, pase)	permít	(permitir)
éxploit	(hazaña)	explóit	(explotar)
óbject	(objeto)	objéct	(objetar)
íncrease	(incremento)	incréase	(aumentar)

EXERCISE D

Repeat the following sentences as accurately as possible after your teacher or the instructor on the tape. Carefully pronounce the stress pattern differences between the italicized words in each sentence.

1. Please **recórd** the **récord**.
2. She was **complétely cómpetent.**
3. We **projéct** that the **próject** will be good.
4. The Sheik was **fífty** with **fiftéen** wives!
5. His hairline began **recéding récently.**
6. The teacher was **contént** with the **cóntent** of the report.
7. He **objécts** to the **óbjects.**
8. I **mistrúst Míster** Smith.
9. She will **presént** you with a **présent.**
10. I **suppóse súpper** will be served.

EXERCISE E

Listen carefully to your teacher or the tape as the following dialogue is presented. Pay careful attention to the stress patterns of the various nouns and verbs in boldface type.

. . . .

ROLANDO:	Welcome to the annual meeting of the **Pérry Próduce Cómpany.** Does **éveryone** remember our **mótto?**
ALL:	Yes. *We prodúce the best **próduce!"***
ROLANDO:	**Árthur,** do you think there will be an **íncrease** in **prófits** next year?
ARTHUR:	Yes **Rolándo.** We will **incréase** our **prófits. Prógress** is our goal!
ROLANDO:	Do you **projéct** having a new **márket?**
ARTHUR:	Yes. Our latest **próject** is the **ímport** of **exótic** fruit.
ROLANDO:	**Reálly!** What will we **impórt?**
ARTHUR:	**Píneapple** from **Hawáii** and dates from the Sahara **Désert.**
ROLANDO:	Did you say **désert** or **dessért?** I love **dessérts!**
ARTHUR:	OK **Rolándo.** I'm so **contént** with the **cóntent** of this **méeting,** I'll treat you to some fresh fruit.
ROLANDO:	Please, **Árthur,** no more fruit! "Health **Dígest**" says fruit is hard to **digést.** I'll have **stráwberry íce-cream!**

. . . .

After listening to the presentation of the dialogue, practice it out loud using proper stress patterns.

SELF-TEST I (Correct answers may be found in Appendix II on page 184.)

Pronounce the following words aloud. Circle the syllable that receives primary stress. **This self-test is not on the tape.**

EXAMPLE: collecting   col ing

1. themselves   them selves
2. birthday   birth day
3. engineer   en gi neer
4. September   Sep tem ber
5. Saturday   Sat ur day

Listen carefully to your teacher or the tape as the following groups of words are presented. Circle the **one** word in each group that has a different stress pattern than the others.

EXAMPLE: connect   control   contain   (constant)

1. agent	annoy	allow	agree
2. upon	until	undo	under
3. protect	program	pronoun	protein
4. token	toaster	today	total
5. supper	sunken	suffer	support
6. explain	extra	excite	exam
7. deepen	deny	devote	degree
8. repair	reason	recent	reader
9. invite	invent	inform	instant
10. open	oppose	over	only

SELF-TEST III   (Correct answers may be found in Appendix II on page 185.)

Read the following sentences aloud. Circle the number of the stressed syllable in each italicized word. **This self-test is not on the tape.**

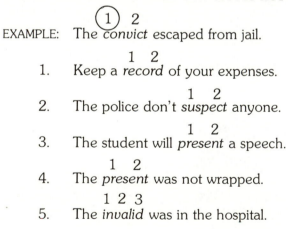

EXAMPLE:
① 2
The *convict* escaped from jail.

1.
1 2
Keep a *record* of your expenses.

2.
1 2
The police don't *suspect* anyone.

3.
1 2
The student will *present* a speech.

4.
1 2
The *present* was not wrapped.

5.
1 2 3
The *invalid* was in the hospital.

Repeat the following poem line by line after your teacher or the instructor on the tape. Circle the number of the stressed syllable in each two-syllable word.

(1) 2   (1) 2 (1) 2
MONEY   by Richard Armour

 1   2
Workers earn it,

  1   2
Spendthrifts burn it,

  1   2
Bankers lend it,

  1   2
Women spend it,

  1 2
Forgers fake it,

1 2
Taxes take it,

1 2
Dying leave it,

      1 2
Heirs receive it,

1 2
Thrifty save it,

 1 2
Misers crave it,

 1   2
Robbers seize it,

      1 2
Rich increase it,

 1   2
Gamblers lose it . . . .

I could use it!

(Reprinted by permission of Branden Press, Inc., 21 Station Street, Brookline Village, MA 02147)

. . . .

After checking your answers in Appendix II, recite the poem again using proper stress patterns. Observe how your teacher or the instructor on the tape consistently emphasizes the noun in each line.

```
*********************************************
```
STRESS WITHIN THE SENTENCE
```
*********************************************
```

SENTENCE STRESS IN ENGLISH

You have already learned that word stress is a major feature of English. Stress patterns go beyond the word level. Just as it is awkward sounding to stress the syllables in a word incorrectly or to stress them all equally, it is unnatural-sounding to stress all the words in a sentence equally or improperly. Effective use of strong and weak emphasis in phrases and sentences will help you achieve your goal of sounding like a native English speaker.

POSSIBLE PRONUNCIATION PROBLEMS FOR THE SPANISH SPEAKER

English sentence level stress patterns are not used the same way as in Spanish. In English, specific words within a sentence are emphasized or spoken louder to make them stand out. (*"It's not **HIS** house; it's **HER** house."*) The Spanish language frequently uses its grammar instead of word stress to convey the same meaning. (*"No es la casa **de él**; es la casa **de ella.**"*) Consequently, you may be confused about when to use strong stress (and when not to use it!) in English sentences. The use of Spanish stress patterns when speaking English will contribute to your foreign accent.

1. You may place the stress on the wrong word. This could:
   a. Completely change the meaning of your statement.

   EXAMPLE: *"He lives in the green **hóuse**"* would sound like *"He lives in the **gréen**house."*

   b. Distort your intended meaning of the sentence.

   EXAMPLE: *"**STEVE'S** my cousin" (not Sam)* would sound like *"Steve's my **COUSIN**" (not my brother).*

2. You may be giving too much or equal stress to unimportant or "function words."

   EXAMPLE: *"I'm in the **HOUSE**"* would sound like *"I'm **IN THE** house."*
   *"He's at the **STORE**"* would sound like ***"HE'S AT THE STORE."***

After reading the explanations and listening to the tape a few times, you will begin to understand the use of English sentence stress patterns. ***YOU SHOULD BE VERY PROUD OF YOURSELF. YOU'VE ALREADY COME A LONG WAY!***

WORDS GENERALLY STRESSED IN SENTENCES: CONTENT WORDS

Content words are the important words in a sentence which convey meaning. We normally **STRESS** content words when speaking. Content words include all the major parts of speech such as nouns, verbs, adjectives, adverbs, and question words.

WORDS GENERALLY UNSTRESSED IN SENTENCES: FUNCTION WORDS

Function Words are the unimportant words in a sentence. They don't carry as much meaning as content words. We normally do **NOT** stress function words when speaking. Function words include the following parts of speech:

a. articles   *(the, a)*
b. prepositions   *(for, of, in, to)*
c. pronouns   *(I, her, him, he, she, you)*
d. conjunctions   *(but, as, and)*
e. helping verbs   *(is, was, are, were, has, can)*

 EXERCISE A

Repeat the following common expressions after your teacher or the instructor on the tape. Be sure to **STRESS** the content words and **NOT** the function words.

1. **sooner** *or* **later**
2. *in a* **moment**
3. *an* **apple** *a* **day**
4. *to* **tell** *the* **truth**
5. *as* **soft** *as a* **kitten**
6. **Silence** *is* **golden**!
7. **Honesty** *is the* **best policy**.
8. **Truth** *is* **stranger** *than* **fiction**.
9. *A* **penny saved** *is a* **penny earned**.
10. *To* **err** *is* **human**; *to* **forgive** *is* **divine**.

STRESSING WORDS TO CLARIFY OR CHANGE MEANING

Sometimes a speaker wants his or her sentence to convey a special meaning which it wouldn't have in the written form. This can be done by stressing a specific word in order to call attention to it. The word that receives the stress depends on the personal motive of the speaker.

EXAMPLE : "I **BOUGHT** ten ties." (I wasn't *given* the ties; I **bought** them.)

EXAMPLE : "I bought ten **TIES.**" (I didn't buy *shirts;* I bought **ties.**)

EXERCISE B

The boldface words in the following questions/responses should receive more emphasis than the others. Repeat them after your teacher or the instructor on the tape.

1 . **Who** likes candy?   **Sam** likes candy.
2. **What** does Sam like?   Sam likes **candy.**
3. Is that **his** car?   No, that's **her** car.
4. Will she **stay**?   No, she'll **leave.**
5. **Where** are you going?   I'm going **home.**
6. **Who's** going home?   **I'm** going home.
7. **When** are you going home?   I'm going home **now.**
8. Did Mary buy a **book**?   No, she bought a **pen.**
9. Did **Mary** buy a book?   No, **Sue** bought a book.
10. Did Mary **buy** a book?   No, Mary **borrowed** a book.

STRESS IN ADJECTIVE/NOUN COMBINATIONS

When you speak, it's important to use words that describe what you are talking about. Words that describe nouns (people, places, or things) are called *adjectives.* When you use adjective/noun combinations, the noun normally receives greater stress.

EXAMPLES: big **DÓG**   good **BOÓK**   pretty **DRÉSS**   nice **BÓY**

By accidentally stressing the adjective, you might mistakenly say a compound noun with a completely different meaning. Your listeners will be confused!

If you stress the adjective instead of the noun:

a. *the green **house** (la casa verde)* becomes *the **green**house (invernáculo)*.

b. *the dark **room** (el cuarto obscuro)* becomes *the **dark**room (el cuarto de revelar)*.

EXERCISE C

Read the following sentence pairs containing adjective/noun combinations and compound words aloud. Be sure to STRESS the NOUN in the Column 1 sentences. **This exercise is not on the tape.**

Sentences with Adjective/Noun Combinations	Sentences with Compound Nouns
The *blue **bird*** is pretty.	The ***blue**bird* is pretty.
We live in the white **house.**	We live in the **White** House.
It's in the *dark **room.***	It's in the **dark**room.
He caught a white **fish.**	He caught a **white**fish.
Look at the *black **bird.***	Look at the **black**bird.

EXERCISE D

Listen carefully to your teacher or the tape as the following dialogue is presented. Pay careful attention to the sentence stress patterns used.

. . . .

JUAN: Anna, who was on the **phone?**
ANNA: My old friend **Mary.**
JUAN: Mary **Jones?**
ANNA: No. Mary **Hall.**
JUAN: I don't know Mary **Hall.** Where is she **from?**
ANNA: She's from **Washington.**
JUAN: Washington the **state** or Washington the **city?**
ANNA: Washington, D.C., our nation's **capital.**
JUAN: Is that where she **lives?**
ANNA: Yes, she still lives in the white **house.**
JUAN: The **White** House? With the **President?**
ANNA: No, silly. The white **house** on **First** Street.
JUAN: What did she **want?**
ANNA: She wants to **come** here.
JUAN: Come **here? When?**
ANNA: In a **week.** She's bringing her black **bird,** her **collie,** her **snakes,** her . . . .
JUAN: **Stop!** She's bringing a **zoo** to **our** house?
ANNA: No, Juan. She's opening a **pet** store here in **town.**

. . . .

After listening to the presentation of the dialogue, practice it aloud. Be sure to **STRESS** the boldface words.

SELF-TEST I

(Correct answers may be found in Appendix II on page 186.)

Read the following sentences aloud. Circle all *Content words* and underline all *Function words*. **This self-test is not on the tape.**

EXAMPLE: The **dogs** are **barking.**

1. Mary is a good friend.
2. Steve is tall and handsome.
3. It's early in the morning.
4. The baby caught a cold.
5. I ate a piece of pie.
6. The store opens at nine.
7. My shoes hurt my feet.
8. Please look for the book.
9. He's leaving in a week.
10. We walked in the snow.

. . . .

After checking your answers in Appendix II, read the sentences again. Be sure to **stress** all *Content words* and **unstress** all *Function words*.

 ## SELF-TEST II

(Correct answers may be found in Appendix II on page 186.)

Your teacher or the instructor on the tape will say EITHER the adjective/noun combination **OR** the compound noun in each of the following pairs. Listen carefully and circle the choice that you hear.

EXAMPLES: a. dark room   **dárk**room
            b. green **hóuse**   greenhouse

1. black **bird**	**black**bird	6. cheap **skates**	**cheap**skates†
2. copper **head**	**copper**head	7. white **fish**	**white**fish
3. blue **bell**	**blue**bell*	8. blue **bird**	**blue**bird
4. light **house**	**light**house	9. black **board**	**black**board
5. white **house**	**White** House	10. green **house**	**green**house

*bluebell = campánula
†cheapskates = tacaños

SELF-TEST III   (Correct answers may be found in Appendix II on page 186.)

In each of the following sentences, the unimportant *or Function words* have been omitted. Fill in the blanks with appropriate *Function words*. **This self-test is not on the tape.**

EXAMPLE: I went _to the_ store.

1. Mary wants _____ cup _____ coffee.
2. _____ show started _____ eight.
3. _____ movie _____ very funny.
4. Sue ate _____ slice _____ cake.
5. We met _____ couple _____ friends _____ mine.

. . . .

After checking your answers in Appendix II, practice reading the sentences aloud. Remember. **DO NOT** stress the *Function words!*

SELF-TEST IV   (Correct answers may be found in Appendix II on page 187.)

Read the following sentences aloud. One word in each sentence should be stressed more than the others. Circle the word that you must stress to clarify the intended meaning of the sentence. Refer back to Exercise D if necessary. **This self-test is not on the tape.**

EXAMPLE   a. Mary (Hall) will visit Juan and Anna. (Not Mary Jones.)
            b. Mary is from (Washington.) (She isn't from New York.)

1. Mary is Anna's friend. (She isn't her cousin.)
2. Juan is married to Anna. (They aren't engaged anymore.)
3. She's from Washington, D.C. (She's not from Washington state.)
4. She lives in the white house. (She doesn't live in the White House.)
5. Her house is on First Street. (It isn't on First Avenue.)
6. Anna and Juan got married three years ago. (Not five years ago.)
7. They own a small home. (They don't rent.)
8. Mary wants to come in a week. (She doesn't want to wait a month.)
9. She'll bring her collie and snakes. (She's not bringing her poodle.)
10. Mary is opening a pet store. (Not a toy store.)

We hope this chapter on stress didn't cause you any stress! You did a beautiful job! It's time to take a break and **_RELAX_** for a while. When you're well rested, move on to the next chapter. **_You'll soon get the RHYTHM!!!_** ⟶

```
*************************************************
```

RHYTHM

```
*************************************************
```

RHYTHM IN ENGLISH

The rhythm of conversational English is more rapid and less precise than formal speech. Every spoken sentence contains syllables or words that receive primary stress. Like the beats in music, strong stresses occur regularly to create a rhythm. Certain words within the sentence must be emphasized while others are spoken more rapidly. This frequently causes sounds to be reduced, changed, or completely omitted. To keep the sentence flowing, words are linked together into phrases and separated by pauses to convey meaning clearly. Effective use of rhythm will help you to achieve more natural-sounding speech.

POSSIBLE PRONUNCIATION PROBLEMS FOR THE SPANISH SPEAKER

In Spanish, all vowels in all syllables are pronounced almost equally. Syllables are rarely lost or reduced as they are in English. It is likely that you are using Spanish conversational rhythm patterns when speaking English. This habit will contribute to a noticeable foreign accent.

1. You may stress each word equally or too precisely.

   EXAMPLE: *"He will **leave** at **three**"* would sound like *"**Hé will leáve át three.**"*

2. You may avoid the use of contractions or reduced forms.

   EXAMPLES: *"I **can't** go"* would sound like *"I **cannot** go."*
   *"He likes **ham'n eggs**"* would sound like *"He likes **ham and eggs.**"*

3. You may insert pauses incorrectly between the words of the sentence, and these will obscure meaning and create a faulty rhythm.

   EXAMPLE: *I don't know Joan"* would sound like *"I don't know, Joan."*

We know this can be slightly confusing at first. *Please do not be concerned! THE EXERCISES IN THIS CHAPTER WILL GET YOU RIGHT INTO THE RHYTHM!!!*

CONTRACTIONS

Contractions are two words that are combined together to form one. Contractions are used frequently in spoken English and are grammatically correct. If you use the full form of the contraction in conversation, your speech will sound stilted and unnatural.

EXAMPLES:

Contraction	*Full Form*
I'll	I will
you're	you are
he's	he is
we've	we have
isn't	is not

EXERCISE A

Read the following pairs of sentences aloud. The first sentence is written in full form, the second contains the contraction. Observe how smooth and natural the second sentence sounds compared with the choppy rhythm of the first sentence. **This exercise is not on the tape.**

1. I am late again.   I'm late again.
2. Mary does not know.   Mary doesn't know.
3. You are next in line.   You're next in line.
4. We have already met.   We've already met.
5. That is right!   That's right!

LINKING AND WORD REDUCTIONS

In conversational English, the words in phrases and short sentences should be linked together as if they were one word.

EXAMPLES: "How are you?" should be pronounced "Howaryou?"
"Do it now!" should be pronounced "Doitnow!"

When words are linked together in this manner, sounds are frequently reduced or omitted completely. (The linking of words and the reductions and omissions of sounds occur **ONLY** in conversational speech. *They are **never** written*.)

EXAMPLES: "*I miss Sam*" = "*I misam*."
                       "*Don't take it.*" = "*Don'take it.*"

This style of speaking (the use of **contractions, linking, and word reductions**) is used by American English speakers in normal conversation and is perfectly acceptable spoken language. Try to use these forms as often as possible when speaking English. **YOU'LL SOON GET THE RHYTHM!!!**

EXERCISE B

Repeat the following phrases and sentences after your teacher or the instructor on the tape. Be sure to blend the words together smoothly and to use reduced forms appropriately.

1.	cream'n sugar	(cream and sugar)
2.	bread'n butter	(bread and butter)
3.	ham'n cheese	(ham and cheese)
4.	pieceəpie	(piece of pie)
5.	I gotə school.	(I go to school.)
6.	He had a cupəcoffee.	(He had a cup of coffee.)
7.	I wanna takeəbreak.	(I want to take a break.)
8.	Seeyəlater.	(See you later.)
9.	Leavmealone.	(Leave me alone.)
10.	Whatimeisit?	(What time is it?)

PHRASING AND PAUSING

A **phrase** is a thought group or a group of words that convey meaning. A **pause** is a brief moment during which the speaker is silent. Sentences should be divided into phrases or thought groups through the use of pauses. The speaker can use a pause to convey or emphasize meaning or simply to take a breath!

EXERCISE C

Read the following sentences aloud. Be sure to PAUSE between each phrase marked by the slanted lines and to blend the words in each phrase. **This exercise is not on the tape.**

1. The phone book // is on the shelf.
2. Steve said // "Sue is gone."
3. "Please help me // Sally"
4. Mr. White // our neighbor // is very nice.
5. I don't agree // and I won't change my mind. ·

SOUND CHANGES

The rapid speech of native American speakers can be difficult for you to understand at times. Sounds in words may run together, disappear, or actually change.

EXAMPLES: *"When did you see her?"* might sound like *"Whenja see-er?"*
"I'll meet you" might sound like *"I'll meetcha."*

It's true that such expressions are not the **"King's English."** In fact, the king would probably turn over in his grave if he were to hear them! Nevertheless, American English speakers use such rhythm patterns in informal, rapid speech. It is important for you to be able to understand these expressions when you hear them.

EXERCISE D

Listen carefully to your teacher or the tape as the following commonly used expressions are presented using the rapid, informal rhythm. (The slow, careful speech form is provided to help you **"SEE"** as well as **"HEAR"** the difference!)

1. Whatsidoin?   (What is he doing?)
2. Whenjarive?   (When did you arrive?)
3. Saniceday!   (It's a nice day!)
4. Nicetəmeetchə.   (Nice to meet you.)
5. Whervyəbeen?   (Where have you been?)

SELF-TEST I (Correct answers may be found in Appendix II on page 187.)

Read the following sentences aloud. Fill in the blanks with the correct contraction. **This self-test is not on the tape.**

EXAMPLES: ***He's***   my favorite teacher. (He is)
                   We're   good friends. (We are)

1. _____ a student. (I am)
2. Lynn _____ play tennis. (does not)
3. _____ seen that movie. (We have)
4. _____ quite right. (You are)
5. His brother _____ come. (cannot)

SELF-TEST II (Correct answers may be found in Appendix II on page 187.)

Read the following sentences aloud, pausing where indicated. Underline the sentence in each pair that is correctly marked for pauses. **This self-test is not on the tape.**

EXAMPLE: <u>I finished my homework // and watched TV.</u>
                 I finished my // homework and watched TV.

1. Meet me at the bus stop // after you're done.
   Meet me at the bus // stop after you're done.

2. Bill Brown the mayor will // speak tonight.
   Bill Brown // the mayor // will speak tonight.

3. Please clean your room // before leaving.
   Please clean your // room before leaving.

4. The truth is I don't // like it.
   The truth is // I don't like it.

5. Cervantes // the famous author // wrote Don Quixote.
   Cervantes the famous author wrote // Don Quixote.

After checking your answers in Appendix II, reread the underlined sentences. Be sure to PAUSE between each phrase marked by the slanted lines and to blend the words in each phrase.

SELF-TEST III (Correct answers may be found in Appendix II on page 188.)

Read the dialogue on the opposite page aloud. Circle all contractions and linked words. In the space below, list these shortened forms and write their full form equivalent. **This self-test is not on the tape.**

Reduced Forms

Howarya? _____

It's _____

_____

_____

_____

_____

_____

_____

_____

_____

_____

_____

_____

_____

_____

_____

Full Form

How are you? _____

It is _____

_____

_____

_____

_____

_____

_____

_____

_____

_____

_____

_____

_____

_____

_____

. . . .

FRANCES BLACK: Hello, this is the Black residence. This is Frances Black speaking.

ELLIE WHITE: (Howarya) Frannie. (It's) Ellie. Doyawanna come over for a cupəcoffee?

FRANCES BLACK: Elinor, I am very sorry. I cannot visit you. I am going to lunch at the Club.

ELLIE WHITE: That's OK. I'm gonna eat at Burger Palace. Why don't we go təthəmovies tonight?

FRANCES BLACK: We will not be able to join you. We have tickets for the opera.

ELLIE WHITE: My husband Sam won't like that. He's more of a wrestling fan. We'll meetchə some other night.

FRANCES BLACK: Elinor, I really have to go now. It has been most pleasant speaking with you.

ELLIE WHITE: I haftə go now too. It's been great talking to you. (Hangs up the phone) Frannie's a nice girl, but she hastə learn to relax!

. . . .

After checking your answers in Appendix II, practice the dialogue with a friend. Be sure to blend the words together smoothly and use the appropriate shortened forms.

FOR AN ENCORE . . . .

Conversation

Record yourself while speaking to a friend by telephone. Listen to your responses carefully. Write down any sentences in which you could have used a contraction instead of the full form. Practice saying the sentences again using the contractions.

```
************************************************
```

INTONATION

```
************************************************
```

DEFINITION

Intonation refers to the use of melody and the rise and fall of the voice when speaking. Each language uses rising and falling pitches differently and has its own distinctive melody and intonation patterns. In fact, babies usually recognize and use the intonation of their native language before they learn actual speech sounds and words.

INTONATION IN ENGLISH

Intonation can determine grammatical meaning as well as the speaker's attitude. It will "tell" whether a person is making a statement or asking a question; it will also indicate if the person is confident, doubtful, shy, annoyed, or impatient. Correct use of intonation is necessary to convey your message correctly and to make you sound like a native English speaker.

POSSIBLE PRONUNCIATION PROBLEMS
FOR THE SPANISH SPEAKER

You already have a head start! Spanish has several of the same basic intonation contours that are found in English. However, English has many more possible variations which change with a speaker's intended meaning, attitude, and emotional state of mind. Without realizing it, you can confuse your listeners by using incorrect English intonation patterns. Examples:

1. Your voice might rise when it should fall. This would:
   a. Change a declarative statement into a question. *(That's Bill's car* would sound like *That's Bill's car?)*
   b. Make you sound doubtful or annoyed.

2. Your voice might stay level when it should either rise or fall. This would:
   a. Make you sound bored or uninterested.
   b. Confuse your listeners into thinking you didn't finish your sentence or question. *(I went home.* would sound like *I went home . . . and . . .)*

Listen to the tape several times before trying to imitate the instructor. With practice, you will soon notice a great improvement. ***KEEP UP THE GOOD WORK!***

PHRASES ENDING WITH A FALLING PITCH

I. Declarative statements

EXAMPLES: Linda is my sister. ↘ He is not going. ↘

II. Questions that require more than a YES/NO response (such question words include *who, what, when, why, where, which, how*)

EXAMPLES: Where is my book? ↘ (On the table. ↘)
When did he leave? ↘ (At three o'clock. ↘)

PHRASES ENDING WITH A RISING PITCH

I. Questions that ask for a YES/NO response (such question words include *can, do, will, would, may, is,* etc.)

EXAMPLES: Will you stay? ↗ (No, I can't. ↘)
Do you like school? ↗ (Yes, I do. ↘)

II. Statements that express doubt or uncertainty

EXAMPLES: I'm not positive. ↗ I think he's coming. ↗

EXERCISE A

Repeat the following statements and questions after the instructor on the tape. Make your voice **FALL** at the end of each of the sentences and questions. Remember, questions that cannot be answered with yes or no take the same **downward** intonation as declarative statements.

1. I have four brothers. ↘
2. He is not my friend. ↘
3. We like ice cream. ↘
4. Tim bought a new car. ↘
5. She likes to play tennis. ↘
6. What is your name? ↘
7. How is your family? ↘
8. Who will drive you home? ↘
9. Why did he leave? ↘
10. Which book is yours? ↘

EXERCISE B

Repeat the following yes/no questions and sample answers after the instructor on the tape. Be sure your voice **rises** ↗ at the end of each question and **falls** ↘ at the end of each response.

YES/NO Questions ↗	**Responses** ↘
1. Can you see?	Yes, I can.
2. Does he play golf?	Yes, he does.
3. May I borrow it?	Yes, you may.
4. Will she help?	No, she won't.
5. Did he arrive?	Yes, he's here now.
6. Is Susan your sister?	No, she's my friend.
7. Have they eaten?	No, they haven't.
8. May I help you?	Yes, please do.
9. Are we leaving?	No, we're staying.
10. Can my friends stay?	Yes, they can.

SOUNDING CONFIDENT INSTEAD OF UNCERTAIN

As was already discussed, a **falling** pitch should be used at the end of declarative statements. It will help you sound confident and sure of yourself. On the other hand, using an **upward** pitch at the end of the same sentences indicates that the speaker is doubtful or uncertain about what he or she is saying.

EXAMPLE: They have 20 children. ↘ (stated as a fact)
They have 20 children. ↗ (stated with doubt or disbelief)

EXERCISE C

Read each of the following statements twice. Use a **falling** ↘ pitch to end the sentences in the first column, and an **upward** ↗ pitch to end the sentences in the second column. *(Notice how the **falling** pitch in the first reading helps you to sound sure of yourself while the **rising** pitch in the second reading makes you sound doubtful or uncertain.)* **This exercise is not on the tape.**

Stated with Certainty ↘	**Stated with Doubt** ↗
1. He ate 25 hot dogs.	He ate 25 hot dogs.
2. The boss gave him a raise.	The boss gave him a raise.
3. You ran 55 miles.	You ran 55 miles.
4. Mike was elected president.	Mike was elected president.
5. It's already 3 o'clock.	It's already 3 o'clock.

INTONATION IN SENTENCES WITH TWO OR MORE PHRASES

Intonation also tells the listener if a speaker has completed the statement/question or whether he or she has more to say. Many sentences are spoken with two or more phrases joined together with such connecting words as *and, if, or, so,* or *but.*

EXAMPLES: *He can sing, but he can't dance.*
             We were hungry, thirsty, and tired.

If your voice drops after the first phrase, your listener will think you are finished with the sentence. To make it clear that you have more to say, you must keep your voice level → before the connecting word and not allow it to fall ↘ until you finish your sentence.

EXAMPLES: *He can sing →, but he can't dance.* ↘
             We were hungry →, thirsty →, and tired. ↘

I. Declarative sentences with two or more phrases

Keep your voice level → before the connecting word and lower it at the end.

EXAMPLES: *I must buy coffee →, tea →, and milk.* ↘
             She speaks French →, but not Spanish. ↘

II. Questions presenting two or more choices

This intonation pattern is the same as for declarative sentences with two or more phrases. Keep your voice level→before the connecting word and lower it when you finish your question. ↘

EXAMPLES: *Would you like cake* →, *or pie?* ↘
Is he leaving tomorrow →, *or Sunday?* ↘

III. Yes/no questions with two or more phrases

Keep your voice level→before the connecting word, and use a rising pitch ↗ at the end of your question.

EXAMPLES: *Will you come* →*if I drive you?* ↗
Did he like the new belt →*and gloves I bought?* ↗

EXERCISE D

Repeat the following multiple phrase statements and questions as accurately as possible after your teacher or the instructor on the tape. (The arrows are there to remind you to use the proper intonation patterns.)

1. May I leave now →, or should I wait? ↘
2. Did you buy a new hat →, or pants? ↘
3. He missed his bus →, but arrived on time. ↘
4. Call me later →, if it's not too late. ↘
5. Will you visit us →, if you're in town? ↗
6. I'll leave early →, so I won't miss the plane. ↘
7. Do you like grapes →, pears →, and plums? ↗
8. He's good at math →, but not spelling. ↘
9. You may stay up late →, if you finish your homework. ↘
10. He went sailing →, swimming →, and fishing. ↘

SELF-TEST I (Correct answers may be found in Appendix II on page 189.)

Listen carefully as the following sentences are presented. The instructor on the tape (or your teacher) will say some of them with certainty and some with doubt, using only intonation to show the difference. On the answer sheet below, circle the sentence you hear.

Sentence #	Stated with Certainty ↘	Stated with Doubt ↗
EXAMPLE :	*Sam will be ready soon.* (circled)	*Sam will be ready soon.*
EXAMPLE :	*The store is open.*	*The store is open.* (circled)

1.	Ron did 90 sit-ups.	Ron did 90 sit-ups.
2.	It only cost ten cents.	It only cost ten cents.
3.	He's really smart.	He's really smart.
4.	She's been married eight times.	She's been married eight times.
5.	You drank two gallons of wine.	You drank two gallons of wine.
6.	The bridge is three miles high.	The bridge is three miles high.
7.	Sue has good taste.	Sue has good taste.
8.	They ate pickles with milk.	They ate pickles with milk.
9.	He read the book in an hour.	He read the book in an hour.
10.	You baked a cake.	You baked a cake.

SELF-TEST II (Correct answers may be found in Appendix II on page 189.)

On the line to the right of each of the following statements/questions, draw the correct intonation arrow. (↘ = voice falls; ↗ = voice rises) **This self-test is not on the tape.**

EXAMPLES: I feel fine. ↘__ (Declarative sentence)
Can you sing? __↗__ (Yes/no question)

1. When's your birthday? ____
2. Did you see my friend? ____
3. How are you? ____
4. I'm fine, thank you. ____
5. Why were you absent? ____

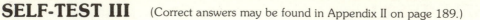

SELF-TEST III   (Correct answers may be found in Appendix II on page 189.)

Listen carefully as the following dialogue is presented. In the blank spaces, draw the correct intonation arrows. (To help you, some intonation arrows are already provided.)

　　　↘ = **Voice falls**　　　↗ = **Voice rises**　　　→ = **Voice stays level**

. . . .

HUSBAND:　Hi, honey. ↘__ What did you do today?___
WIFE:　I went shopping. ___
HUSBAND:　You went shopping? ___ Again? ↗__
WIFE:　Yes. ↘__ The store had a big sale. ↘__ Everything was half price. ___
HUSBAND:　What did you buy now? ___
WIFE:　I bought this blouse for thirty dollars. ___ Isn't it stunning? ___
HUSBAND:　Yes, it's stunning. ___ I'm the one that's stunned. ↘__
WIFE:　Do you like the green hat →__ or the red one? ___
HUSBAND:　I like the cheaper one. ___
WIFE:　I also bought a belt, ___ scarf, →__ dress, ___ and shoes. ___
HUSBAND:　Stop it! ___ I'm afraid to hear any more. ___ Do we have any money left? ___
WIFE:　Yes, dear, we have lots of money left. ↘__ I saved two hundred dollars on my new clothes, ___ so I bought you a set of golf clubs. ___
HUSBAND:　Really? ↗__ I always said you were a great shopper! ___

. . . .

After checking your answers in Appendix II, practice the dialogue out loud. Be sure to use the correct intonation patterns as indicated by the intonation arrows.

FOR AN ENCORE ....

Listening

Listen as a native English speaker tells a joke. It may be a television personality or someone you know personally. Observe the speaker's use of vocal melody and intonation patterns which make the joke effective.

Conversation

Practice the joke you heard and analyzed for intonation. Tape yourself saying the joke; be sure to use the proper intonation—*ESPECIALLY ON THE PUNCH LINE!* When you feel confident, tell the joke to three different people.

THAT'S ALL FOLKS!!!

Believe it or not, you have just finished reading the LAST chapter in the book. **CONGRATULATIONS!!** You've earned your degree in **English Pronunciation for Spanish Speakers: Vowels.** It was worth all that hard work, wasn't it? **But—*education is a continuing process. Although we've stressed it all along, we'll say it again:* THE MORE YOU PRACTICE, THE BETTER YOU WILL BECOME.**

   Daniel Webster once said, "If all my possessions were taken from me with one exception, I would choose to keep the power of communication, for by it I would soon regain all the rest."

   SO—keep practicing and CLEAR, EFFECTIVE COMMUNICATION WILL BE YOURS FOREVER.

Best of luck always,

Lillian Poms

Paulette Dale

Lillian Poms and Paulette Dale

```
*******************************************
```

APPENDIX I:
TO THE TEACHER

```
*******************************************
```

WELCOME TO THE CHALLENGE! You recommended **English Pronunciation for Spanish Speakers** to your students because you are committed to helping them improve their pronunciation of English. This is a difficult task. But—it's NOT impossible. Teaching and learning English pronunciation can be difficult, tedious work. It can also be more fun than you ever imagined possible! (In our accent reduction classes, there have been countless occasions when we, along with our students, have laughed long and hard enough for the tears to roll!)

Some of you are already experienced ESL or speech instructors and/or speech pathologists involved in teaching foreign accent reduction classes, and you already employ a variety of effective techniques with your students. *PLEASE*—share some of your most successful ones with us. *AND*—we invite you to let us know how you like *OUR* suggestions. **We truly look forward to hearing from you!**

Some of you are new at teaching English pronunciation to non-native speakers. **DON'T WORRY!** An enthusiastic attitude and genuine desire to learn with your students will be more valuable than years of experience. As you'll quickly realize, the **English Pronunciation for Spanish Speakers** program provides you with an easy-to-follow, systematic approach to teaching English pronunciation.

BREAKING THE ICE

Teaching foreign accent reduction can and SHOULD be fun for all concerned. At first, students will invariably be apprehensive and self-conscious about taking such a course and "exposing" their speech patterns in front of you and their peers. The time you spend trying to alleviate their initial concerns will be time well spent. We recommend:

1. Using the first class meeting to discuss the positive aspects of "accents" in general. Elaborate on the information presented on page 2 in "To the Student."

2. Emphasizing that accent reduction is NOT the losing of one's culture or heritage, but the improvement of a skill, as is the ability to play the piano, guitar, or tennis! Our students relate well to such analogies.

3. Describing your own embarrassing mistakes or those of other native Americans when speaking a foreign language. Our students laugh heartily at our examples and are comforted by the thought that we, too, experience pronunciation difficulties when speaking our second language.

HEARING THE SOUNDS

Advise your students that their initial difficulty in hearing the various vowel sounds is perfectly normal. Non-native speakers of English frequently have difficulty recognizing sounds absent in their native language. (Scholes [1968] found that the sound system of one's native language will influence his or her perception of English phonemes.) Your students will overcome this initial "deafness" to specific sounds after directed auditory discrimination practice. If possible, ask your school nurse, speech pathologist, or local public health department to administer a quick, routine hearing screening to each of your students. This will dissolve their concerns (and yours!) about any possibility of hearing loss.

ACCENT ANALYSIS

The *ACCENT ANALYSIS* that follows should be used at the beginning of the **English Pronunciation for Spanish Speakers** program. Record each student (or have them record themselves at home) reading the Accent Analysis Sentences. Each group of sentences is designed to survey the students' pronunciation of a specific target vowel or diphthong. Encourage them to read the sentences in a natural, conversational voice. The accent analysis should be used again when your students complete the program. This will help you (and them!) measure their progress.

Now you are ready to listen to your students' tapes and do a written survey of their vowel, diphthong, and word-stress difficulties. The Teacher's Record and Summary of Errors forms on pages 156–158 provide a place to record the results.

As each group of sentences is read, listen only to the pronunciation of the **target sound**. Ignore all other errors. While a student is reading, follow along sentence by sentence on the **Teacher's Record Form**. Circle all target words that are mispronounced. On the line above the mispronounced target word, record the error. Use any marking (e.g., phonetic or dictionary symbol) that is meaningful to you. You can then complete the **Summary of Errors Form** on page 158 at your leisure.

EXAMPLE: Your student substitutes [aʊ] (as in "out") for [ɔ] in sentence 9 target words "author" and "audience," and [oʊ] (as in "no") in "office" and "boring." You might record the errors as follows:

    au   ou   au

[ɔ] 9. The **author** gave a **long talk** in the **office**. The **small audience**

              ou

    thought it was **boring.**

On the **Summary of Errors** form, you might make the following notations:

VOWELS	**Correct**	**Error**	**Comments**
			Errors seem related to
9. [ɔ] as in *ALL*	—	[aʊ] & [oʊ] for [ɔ]	*spelling patterns*

ACCENT ANALYSIS SENTENCES

1. Please believe that sweet peas and beans are good to eat. Eat them at least twice a week.

2. Tim's sister swims a little bit. It keeps her fit, slim, and trim.

3. Ten times seven is seventy. Seven times eleven is seventy-seven.

4. Many animals inhabit Africa. Africa has camels, giraffes, parrots, and bats.

5. Doctors say jogging is good for the body. Lots of starch causes heart problems.

6. Who flew to the moon? Numerous lunar flights are in the news. We'll soon put a man on Jupiter and Pluto.

7. Would you look for my cookbook? It should be full of hints for good cookies and pudding.

8. The southern governor is Republican. The public election was fun. He won by one hundred votes.

9. The author gave a long talk in the office. The small audience thought it was boring.

10. Nurses do worthy work. They certainly deserve a word of praise.

11. Labor Day is in September. Workers are honored.

12. Maine is a state in the northern United States. It's a great place for a vacation.

13. The North Pole is close to the Arctic Ocean. It's known for polar bears, snow, and severe cold.

14. Owls are now found throughout the world. They avoid crowds and make loud sounds.

15. Eyesight is vital for a normal life. I prize mine highly.

16. The auto industry is a loyal employer in Detroit. People enjoy their choice of cars.

17. Africa, Asia, Australia, South America, and Europe comprise five of the continents. North America is the other continent.

18. I have televisions in the bedroom, living room, and dining room. The programs about detectives and hospitals are my favorite.

TEACHER'S RECORD FORM

TARGET VOWELS

[i]   1.   **Please believe** that **sweet peas** and **beans** are good to **eat.
Eat** them at **least** twice a **week.**

[ɪ]   2.   **Tim's sister swims** a **little bit. It** keeps her **fit, slim,** and **trim.**

[ɛ]   3.   **Ten** times **seven** is **seventy. Seven** times **eleven** is **seventy-seven.**

[æ]   4.   Many **animals inhabit Africa. Africa has camels, giraffes, parrots,** and **bats.**

[a]   5.   **Doctors** say **jogging** is good for the **body. Lots** of **starch** causes **heart problems.**

[u]   6.   **Who flew to** the **moon? Numerous lunar** flights are in the **news.** We'll **soon** put a man on **Jupiter** and **Pluto.**

[ʊ]   7.   **Would** you **look** for my **cookbook?** It **should** be **full** of hints for **good cookies** and **pudding.**

[ʌ]   8.   The **southern governor** is **Republican.** The **public** election **was fun.** He **won** by **one hundred** votes.

[ɔ]   9.   The **author** gave a **long talk** in the **office.** The **small audience thought** it was **boring.**

[ɝ] 10. **Nurses** do **worthy work.** They **certainly deserve** a **word** of praise.

[ɚ] 11. **Labor** Day is in **September. Workers** are **honored.**

TARGET DIPHTHONGS

[eɪ] 12. Maine is a state in the northern United States. It's a great place for a vacation.

[oʊ] 13. The North Pole is close to the Arctic Ocean. It's known for polar bears, snow, and severe cold.

[aʊ] 14. Owls are now found throughout the world. They avoid crowds and make loud sounds.

[aɪ] 15. Eyesight is vital for a normal life. I prize mine highly.

[ɔɪ] 16. The auto industry is a loyal employer in Detroit. People enjoy their choice of cars.

WORD STRESS

[ə] 17. Africa, Asia, Australia, South America, and Europe comprise five of the continents. North America is the other continent.

18. I have televisions in the bedroom, living room, and dining room. The programs about detectives and hospitals are my favorite.*

---

*The boldface letters indicate the syllable that should receive primary stress. If the student errs on a target word, circle the incorrectly stressed syllable.

Student's Name _____

Date: _____

Summary of Errors

VOWELS	**Correct**	**Error**		**Comments**
1. [i] as in *ME*	_____	_____	for [i]	_____
2. [ɪ] as in *IT*	_____	_____	for [ɪ]	_____
3. [ɛ] as in *EGG*	_____	_____	for [ɛ]	_____
4. [æ] as in *AT*	_____	_____	for [æ]	_____
5. [a] as in *HOT*	_____	_____	for [a]	_____
6. [u] as in *YOU*	_____	_____	for [u]	_____
7. [ʊ] as in *COOK*	_____	_____	for [ʊ]	_____
8. [ʌ] as in *UP*	_____	_____	for [ʌ]	_____
9. [ɔ] as in *ALL*	_____	_____	for [ɔ]	_____
10. [ɝ] as in *FIRST*	_____	_____	for [ɝ]	_____
11. [ɚ] as in *FATHER*	_____	_____	for [ɚ]	_____

DIPHTHONGS

	Correct	**Error**		**Comments**
12. [eɪ] as in *ATE*	_____	_____	for [eɪ]	_____
13. [oʊ] as in *NO*	_____	_____	for [oʊ]	_____
14. [aʊ] as in *OUT*	_____	_____	for [aʊ]	_____
15. [aɪ] as in *MY*	_____	_____	for [aɪ]	_____
16. [ɔɪ] as in *BOY*	_____	_____	for [ɔɪ]	_____

WORD STRESS

Correct **Incorrect** (Does not reduce in unstressed syllables)

17. [ə] as in *SODA* _____ _____

18. Is stress placed on the wrong syllable of words of more than one syllable?

Errors: _____

OTHER OBSERVATIONS:

USING THE MANUAL FOR CLASSROOM INSTRUCTION

Whether you are an instructor of ESL, speech, or accent reduction, or a speech pathologist, you will find **English Pronunciation for Spanish Speakers** completely adaptable for classroom or clinical use. The exercises and self-tests in the manual have been tested in the classroom and have proven to be effective with non-native speakers of English striving to improve their American English pronunciation. The manual is so complete that it eliminates the need for you to spend endless hours preparing drill materials. The following are some suggestions to help you use the manual effectively.

To the Student

Read this section first to familiarize yourself with the organization and content of the manual.

Sequence of Material Presentation

The order of sound presentation is flexible. The integrity of the program will remain intact if you assign the chapters in a sequence of your own choosing. Your personal teaching philosophy, available time, and students' specific needs should dictate what you teach first. Many students will not have difficulty with all the sounds. Consequently, you may wish to skip some chapters completely and spend more time on the ***"real troublemakers"*** (like [I] as in "it" or [ʊ] as in "cook")!

A Key to Pronouncing the Vowels of American English

In this section you are introduced to the International Phonetic Alphabet. Don't be concerned if you are currently unfamiliar with the phonetic symbols. Each symbol is introduced and explained one at a time. You will learn them easily and gradually as you progress through the program with your students. Refer back to the **Key to Pronouncing the Vowels of American English** (page 7) when you need to refresh your memory.

Adaptation of Material

The material presented in each chapter can be adapted easily. If your students require more drill at the sentence level before progressing to dialogues or paragraphs, focus your attention on the appropriate exercises; defer presentation of more difficult activities to a later time.

Self-Tests

The self-tests can be used in a variety of ways: (1) You can present the tests as described in the manual to evaluate your students' progress; (2) You can use them as both **PRE** and **POST** tests to more precisely measure their gains; (3) You might prefer to divide your students into "teams" to complete the tests as a group rather than individually; or (4) You can assign the self-tests as "homework" to encourage out-of-class practice.

For an Encore

The activities in this section can easily be expanded for classroom use. The diversity of these assignments will certainly liven up the regular classroom routine. For example, in the [i] and [ɪ] chapter, the students are asked to make several social introductions using phrases pronounced with the target sounds. This activity could be employed in the classroom by having students introduce themselves to each other.

SUPPLEMENTARY ACTIVITIES

As an extra bonus, here are some additional in-class activities to vary your presentation of the material in the manual.

Objective: To increase the student's ability to recognize the target vowel auditorily.

Activity 1: Read Exercise A words orally in mixed order. Have the students identify the target vowel as occurring in either the initial, medial, or final position.

Activity 2: Read phrase and sentence exercises orally. Have the students list all the words containing the target vowel.

Objective: To increase the student's ability to discriminate between the target vowel and his or her error.

Activity 1: Use minimal pairs exercises/self-tests (e.g., Exercise C on page 30). Create word pairs such as ***bit—bit and bit—beat.*** Have the students identify the words in each pair as being the SAME or DIFFERENT.

Activity 2: Read orally from the minimal pairs exercises. Vary the order of the words (***bit—beat, seat—sit***). Have the students indicate whether they heard the target vowel in the first or second word.

Activity 3: Give a "spelling test." Read individual words from the minimal pairs exercises. Have your students write the words as you say them. This is a sure way to determine if they are hearing the target sound.

Activity 4: Read the phrase and sentence exercises orally. Alternate between imitating a student's typical error and pronouncing the target sound correctly. Have your students determine whether or not the words in the phrases and sentences have been produced accurately.

Objective: To increase the student's ability to produce the target vowel.

Activity 1: Have your students role-play using the self-test dialogues at the end of each chapter.

Activity 2: Play a memory game using the word lists in the manual. Ask one student to complete a sentence with a word containing the target vowel. The next student must repeat the sentence and add another word with the target sound.

Example for target vowel [ɪ]: "I'm going on a ***trip*** and I ***will bring*** a ***pin, winter*** coat, ***guitar,*** _____,. . . ."

With all of these suggestions and the activities described in the manual, your students will be kept occupied and learning throughout the course!

APPENDIX II: ANSWERS

ANSWERS TO SELF-TEST I ON PAGE 14.

1. (steam)	6. Christmas	11. pencil	16. (agree)
2. stem	7. holiday	12. (season)	17. been
3. (easy)	8. difficult	13. winter	18. (bean)
4. window	9. (three)	14. spring	19. ice
5. (Easter)	10. six	15. (even)	20. (meat)

ANSWERS TO SELF-TEST II ON PAGE 14.

1. bead	(great)	leave	tea
2. (eight)	either	believe	niece
3. scene	(women)	these	even
4. need	(been)	sleep	thirteen
5. police	thief	machine	(vision)
6. (pretty)	wheat	sweet	cream
7. people	(bread)	deal	east
8. (tin)	teen	steam	receive
9. leave	(live)	leaf	lease
10. steep	Steve	easy	(still)

ANSWERS TO SELF-TEST I ON PAGE 17.

1. fifty	sixty	(eighteen)	six
2. window	sill	widow	(wipe)
3. (freedom)	sympathy	simple	symbol
4. building	(smile)	little	guitar
5. pistol	(resign)	fiddle	whistle
6. quit	criminal	(crime)	brittle
7. (sheep)	flip	tickle	fifteen
8. pretty	been	(feet)	fit
9. business	women	(leave)	lift
10. (piece)	pity	typical	tips

ANSWERS TO SELF-TEST II ON PAGE 17.

1.	① 2	(sit	seat)		6.	1 ②	(beat	bit)
2.	1 ②	(feet	fit)		7.	1 ②	(neat	knit)
3.	① 2	(fist	feast)		8.	① 2	(hit	heat)
4.	1 ②	(eat	it)		9.	1 ②	(sheep	ship)
5.	① 2	(list	least)		10.	① 2	(bin	bean)

ANSWERS TO SELF-TEST I ON PAGE 19.

1.	field (filled)		6. (team) Tim
2.	(bean) bin		7. (sleep) slip
3.	neat (knit)		8. green (grin)
4.	deal (dill)		9. heel (hill)
5.	beat (bit)		10. (week) wick

ANSWERS TO SELF-TEST II ON PAGE 19.

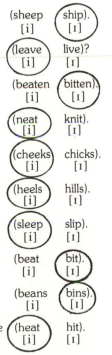

1.	They cleaned the	(sheep [i]	(ship). [ɪ]
2.	Will he	(leave [i]	live)? [ɪ]
3.	The boy was	(beaten [i]	(bitten). [ɪ]
4.	His clothes are	(neat [i]	knit). [ɪ]
5.	She has plump	(cheeks [i]	chicks). [ɪ]
6.	I like low	(heels [i]	hills). [ɪ]
7.	The children will	(sleep [i]	slip). [ɪ]
8.	I heard every	(beat [i]	(bit). [ɪ]
9.	They stored the	(beans [i]	(bins). [ɪ]
10.	Everyone talks about the	(heat [i]	hit). [ɪ]

　　　　　　[ɪ] [ɪ]　　　　[i]
1.　Take a **dip in** the **deep** water.

　　　　　　[ɪ]　　　[ɪ]　　　　　[i]
2.　They **picked Tim** for the **team**.

　　　　[i]　　　[i]　　　　[i]　　　[i]
3.　**Please beat** the **sweet cream**.

　　　　[i] [ɪ]　[ɪ] [ɪ]　　　[i]
4.　**She will sit in** the **seat**.

　　　　　　[i]　　　　[ɪ]　　　[ɪ]
5.　The **heat** wave **hit** the **city**.

　　　[i]　　　　[ɪ]　　　　　　[i]
6.　**Jean** has **been** cooking **beans**.

　　　　　　[i]　　　[ɪ] [ɪ]
7.　His pet **eel** is **still ill**!

　　　　　　[i]　　　[ɪ] [ɪ]　[ɪ]
8.　At **least** my **list is finished**.

　　[ɪ] [i]　[i]　　　　[i]
9.　**Is he** at **ease** on **skis**?

　　　　[i]　[ɪ]　　　　[ɪ]　　[i]
10.　**These slippers** don't **fit** my **feet**.

JIM:　　Hi, Tina! Do you have a **minute**?

TINA:　Yes, Jim. What is it?

JIM:　　My sister is in the city on business. We will eat dinner out tonight. Can you recommend a place to eat?

TINA:　There is a fine seafood restaurant on Fifth Street. The fish is fresh and the shrimp is great. But it isn't cheap!

JIM:　　That's OK. It will be "feast today, famine tomorrow"! I'll have to eat "frijoles" the rest of the week!

164

ANSWERS TO SELF-TEST I ON PAGE 25.

(steak)   lettuce   (mayonnaise)   cereal
bread   (raisins)   melon   bananas
(cake)   (tomatoes)   (bacon)   (baking soda)
(potatoes)   crackers   peas   ice cream
(grapes)   celery   (gravy)   carrots
toothpaste   peas   squash   (paper plates)

ANSWERS TO SELF-TEST II ON PAGE 25.

1. (1) 2 3 (Kate cat   cot)   6. (1) 2 3 (rate rat   rot)
2. 1 (2) 3 (can   cane con)   7.   1 (2) 3 (ran   rain wren)
3. 1 2 (3) (pen   pan   pain)   8. (1) 2 3 (late let   lot)
4. 1 (2) 3 (foot fate fat)   9.   1 (2) 3 (calm came comb)
5. (1) 2 3 (mate mat   met)   10. (1) 2 3 (wait what wet)

ANSWERS TO SELF-TEST III ON PAGE 26.

1. (practice)   plate   play   place
2. stay   aid   (plaid)   raid
3. neighbor   freight (height)   eighty
4. (head)   great   break   came
5. shave   (any)   staple   pays
6. (America)   Asia   Spain   Maine
7. laid   crayon   (seven)   tame
8. great   grace   grey   (greedy)
9. obtain   awake   create   (breakfast)
10. snake   obey   (breath)   complain

ANSWERS TO SELF-TEST IV ON PAGE 26.

(Babe) Ruth was a (famous) (baseball) (player.) He was born and (raised) in an orphanage in Baltimore. He first (played) for the Boston Red Sox but was (later) (traded) to the New York Yankees. He (made) 714 home runs and (became) a (baseball) legend. He was (named) to the (Baseball) Hall of (Fame.) The last team he (played) for was the Boston (Braves.) He died in (1948.) Many (say) he was the (greatest) (player) of his (day.)

165

ANSWERS TO SELF-TEST I ON PAGE 31.

1. Dec(e)mber
2. rej(e)ct
3. (e)very
4. (e)levator
5. s(e)venteen

6. el(e)ven
7. rem(e)mber
8. r(e)ference
9. s(e)cretary
10. t(e)lephone

ANSWERS TO SELF-TEST II ON PAGE 31.

1. any — (crazy) — anywhere — many
2. (paper) — letter — send — pencil
3. seven — eleven — (eight) — twenty
4. health — (wreath) — breath — wealth
5. (reading) — ready — already — head
6. present — precious — (preview) — president
7. November — February — September — (April)
8. guess — guest — (cues) — question
9. thread — threat — fresh — (theater)
10. (mean) — meant — meadow — met

ANSWERS TO SELF-TEST III ON PAGE 32.

1. C (I) (He went to **bad** early.)
2. C (I) (The opposite of east is **waste.**)
3. (C) I (She is my **best** friend.)
4. C (I) (The **pan** ran out of ink.)
5. (C) I (This is the **end** of the test!)
6. C (I) (Please **sand** the letter.)
7. (C) I (Did you **sell** your car?)
8. C (I) (**Raid** is my favorite color.)
9. C (I) (Put salt and **paper** on the salad.)
10. (C) I (Can you **guess** the right answer?)

166

ANSWERS TO SELF-TEST IV ON PAGE 33.

MS. NELSON: "**Nelson Temporary Help.**" Ms. Nelson speaking. Can I help you?
MR. PEREZ: Yes, this is Pepe Perez. I need a temporary secretary.
MS. NELSON: What kind of secretary do you need?
MR. PEREZ: The BEST! That means well educated and with excellent clerical skills.
MS. NELSON: Anything else?
MR. PEREZ: Yes, I like pretty secretaries with good legs. Get what I mean?
MS. NELSON: Yes, I do. I have the best secretary for you. I'll send one Wednesday at ten.
MR. PEREZ: Thanks. It's been a pleasure talking to you.
MS. NELSON: Evelyn, get me Ted Benson's file. He's an excellent secretary and has very good legs!!!

ANSWERS TO SELF-TEST I ON PAGE 37.

1. (1) 2 3 (rack   rock   wreck)   6. (1) 2 3 (laughed   left   loft)
2. 1 2 (3) (lake   lock   lack)   7. 1 2 (3) (sneak   snake   snack)
3. (1) 2 3 (add   aid   Ed)   8. 1 (2) 3 (paste   past   pest)
4. 1 (2) 3 (pot   pat   pet)   9. (1) 2 3 (hat   hot   hate)
5. 1 2 (3) (top   tape   tap)   10. 1 (2) 3 (made   mad   mod)

ANSWERS TO SELF-TEST II ON PAGE 37.

Dear Mom and Dad,

At last we are in San Francisco. It's a fabulous city! As we stand at the top of Telegraph Hill we can see Alcatraz. We plan to catch a cable car and visit Grant Avenue in Chinatown. After that, we'll have tea in the Japanese Gardens. Yesterday we drank wine in Napa Valley. We also passed through the National Park. Our last stop is Disneyland in Los Angeles. We'll be back next Saturday.

Love,

Gladys

P.S. We need cash. Please send money fast!

ANSWERS TO SELF-TEST III ON PAGE 38.

1. p a r a d i s e
2. A f r i c a
3. C a l i f o r n i a
4. f a s c i n a t e
5. A l a s k a

6. a t t a c k
7. S a t u r d a y
8. C a n a d a
9. D a l l a s
10. p a c k a g e

ANSWERS TO SELF-TEST I ON PAGE 42.

1. 1 ②③ 3 (rub   rob   robe)   6. ① 2 3 (fond   fund   phoned)
2. ① 2 3 (hot   hat   hut)   7. 1 ② 3 (stack   stock   stuck)
3. 1 2 ③. (pope   pup   pop)   8. ① 2 3 (cot   cut   caught)
4. 1 ② 3 (gut   got   goat)   9. 1 ② 3 (cup   cop   cope)
5. 1 ② 3 (note   not   nut)   10. ① 2 3 (mod   mud   mowed)

ANSWERS TO SELF-TEST II ON PAGE 42.

1. V e r m ⓞ n t   6. H ⓞ l l a n d
2. M ⓞ s c o w   7. M o r ⓞ c c o
3. B a h ⓐ m a s   8. C a r ⓐ c a s
4. S c ⓞ t l a n d   9. C h i c ⓐ g o
5. N e v ⓐ d a   10. Ⓞ s l o

ANSWERS TO SELF-TEST III ON PAGE 43.

(condor)   (collie)   leopard   (llama)
cat   (crocodile)   elephant   sea (otter)
(fox)   tiger   (hippopotamus)   (dolphin)
(iguana)   kangaroo   (lobster)   (octopus)
parrot   (rhinoceros)   (opossum)   lion

ANSWERS TO SELF-TEST IV ON PAGE 43.

· ·

The (Constitution)

The United States (Constitution) is the basis of our (democracy.) Much (compromise) was necessary before the (constitution) was (adopted.) Some (modifications) to the (constitution) caused (problems) which were (resolved) by forming two houses in (Congress.) Other countries change their (constitutions) when a new (politician) takes office. The United States (Constitution) has been (constant) but (responsive) to change. We thank our founding (fathers) for this (remarkable) (document.)

· ·

ANSWERS TO REVIEW TEST I ON PAGE 47.

1. Leave the car in the   (shed   (shade).
        [ɛ]·   [eɪ]

2. Do you know what was   (sad   (said).
        [æ]   [ɛ]

3. We need more   (paper)   pepper).
        [eɪ].   [ɛ]

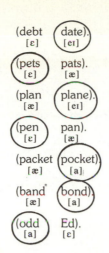

4. Please clear that   (debt   (date)).
                               [ɛ]   [eɪ]

5. Children like   (pets)   pats).
                              [ɛ]   [æ]

6. They made the   (plan   (plane)).
                              [æ]   [eɪ]

7. I bought a new   (pen)   pan).
                              [ɛ]   [æ]

8. The note is in the   (packet   (pocket)).
                              [æ]   [a]

9. Did she pay for the   (band   (bond)).
                              [æ]   [a]

10. I think it was   (odd)   Ed).
                              [a]   [ɛ]

ANSWERS TO REVIEW TEST II ON PAGE 48.

[eɪ] as in *ATE*	[ɛ] as in *EGG*	[æ] as in *HAT*	[a] as in *HOT*
freight	egg	match	watch
April	bell	vast	blonde
plane	guess	apple	shock
steak	any	half	part
staple	said	can't	fox
veil	help	laugh	top
name	friend	plaid	wasp
aid			stop

ANSWERS TO REVIEW TEST III ON PAGE 49.

1.   not   (The party is at three, *nut* at four.)
2.   steak   (I eat *stock* medium rare.)
3.   headache   (Take aspirin for your *hadache.*)
4.   watch   (*My witch* tells perfect time.)
5.   late   (It's better to be early than *let.*)
6.   send   (Please *sand* the letter air mail.)
7.   pet   (He has a dog as a *pot.*)
8.   cat   (I have a Siamese *cot* and goldfish.)
9.   tastes   (The apple pie *tests* good.)
10.   weight   (If you eat too much, you'll gain *wet!*)

ANSWERS TO REVIEW TEST IV ON PAGE 50.

[1] [2]   [1]   [2]   [1]
He was a famous president of the United States. He was elected in eighteen sixty. He was

[4] [1]   [1]   [1]   [3]
known as Honest Abe. He freed the slaves. The name of this man is *Abraham Lincoln* .

[1]   [1]   [1]   [3]   [2]
She was a famous queen. She reigned in Spain and married Ferdinand. She sent

[4]   [4]   [4]   [2]   [2]   [1]
Columbus to a large new continent. This voyage started the settlement of America. The name of

[1]
this lady is *Queen Isabella* .

[1]   [1]   [1]   [4]   [4]
He was a famous playwright. He came from England and is probably the most popular

[4]   [3] [1]   [2]   [3]   [4]   [2]
writer in the world. His dramas have been translated into every language. Shylock, Macbeth,

[2]   [2]   [1]   [3]
and Henry VI are among his many characters. The name of this man is *William Shakespeare*

ANSWERS TO SELF-TEST I ON PAGE 54.

1. 1 2 ③ (look   look   Luke)   6. ① 2 3 (wooed   wave   would)
2. 1 ② 3 (cook   kook   cook)   7. ① 2 3 (stewed stood   stayed)
3. ① 2 3 (fool   fall   full)   8. 1 ② 3 (toll   tool   tall)
4. ① 2 3 (mood   mud   made)   9. 1 2 ③ (pull   pole   pool)
5. ① 2 3 (suit   sat   soot)   10. 1 ② 3 (skull   school scale)

ANSWERS TO SELF-TEST I ON PAGE 57.

1. C ① (You **shooed** drive carefully.)
2. © I (I like chocolate chip **cookies**)
3. C ① (He **stewed** on the ladder.)
4. C ① (The carpenter sawed the **wooed.**)
5. C ① (The pool was **fool** of water.)
6. © I (The police caught the **crook**.)
7. © I (The gun has **bullets**.)
8. C ① (Please don't **pool** my hair.)
9. © I (I like coffee with **sugar**.)
10. © I (He broke his left **foot**.)

170

ANSWERS TO SELF-TEST I ON PAGE 59.

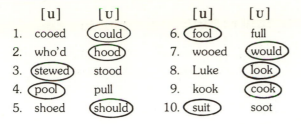

	[u]	[ʊ]		[u]	[ʊ]
1.	cooed	(could)	6.	(fool)	full
2.	who'd	(hood)	7.	wooed	(would)
3.	(stewed)	stood	8.	Luke	(look)
4.	(pool)	pull	9.	kook	(cook)
5.	shoed	(should)	10.	(suit)	soot

ANSWERS TO SELF-TEST II ON PAGE 59.

1.	1 2 ③ (look look Luke)	6.	1 2 ③ (wooed wooed would)
2.	1 ② 3 (cook kook cook)	7.	① 2 3 (stewed stood stood)
3.	1 2 ③ (fool fool full)	8.	1 2 ③ (could could cooed)
4.	① 2 3 (pull pool pool)	9.	① 2 3 (wooed wood wood)
5.	1 2 ③ (suit suit soot)	10.	① 2 3 (hood who'd who'd)

ANSWERS TO SELF-TEST III ON PAGE 60.

1.   [u]   [ʊ]   [u]
   Too many ***cooks*** spoil the ***soup!***
2.   [ʊ]   [ʊ] [u]
   There ***should*** be a ***full moon***.
3.   [ʊ]   [ʊ] [ʊ]
   Mr. ***Brooks*** is ***good looking***.
4.   [u]   [ʊ]   [u]
   June is a ***good*** month to ***move***.
5.   [ʊ]   [ʊ]   [u]
   The ***butcher cooked*** a ***goose***.
6.   [u]   [ʊ]   [ʊ]
   The ***news bulletin*** was ***misunderstood***.
7.   [u]   [u]   [u] [u]
   Did ***you choose*** a pair of ***new shoes?***
8.   [u]   [u]   [u] [ʊ]
   Lucy had a ***loose tooth pulled***.
9.   [u]   [ʊ]   [u] [ʊ]
   Students should read ***good books***.
10.   [u]   [ʊ]   [u] [u]
   The ***room*** is ***full*** of ***blue balloons***.

ANSWERS TO SELF-TEST IV ON PAGE 61.

· ·

Harry (Houdini) was a magician known (throughout) the world. He (could) (remove) himself from chains and ropes and could walk (through) walls! (Houdini) was born in (Budapest,) Hungary. He (moved) to (New) York when he was twelve and (soon) took up magic. (Rumors) spread that (Houdini) had (supernatural) powers. However, he was (truthful) and stated that his tricks could be understood by all (humans! (Houdini) is an idol for all "would-be" magicians.

· ·

171

ANSWERS TO SELF-TEST I ON PAGE 66.

COCKTAILS
Martini   Wine   (Rum Punch)

APPETIZERS
(Stuffed Mushrooms)   Shrimp Cocktail   Melon

SOUPS
Gazpacho   (French Onion)   Clam Chowder

SALAD
Hearts of Lettuce   Caesar   (Tomato and Cucumber)

VEGETABLES
(Buttered Corn)   Baked Potato   Carrots

ENTREES
Arroz con Pollo   Prime Ribs   (Roast Duck)

BREADS
Italian Bread   (Hot Muffins)   Garlic Rolls

DESSERTS
(Pumpkin Pie)   Vanilla Pudding   Ice Cream

BEVERAGES
Coffee   Milk   (Cup of Tea)

ANSWERS TO SELF-TEST II ON PAGE 67.

1. (C)   I   (I like toast and **butter**.)
2. C   (I)   (I wish you good **lock**.)
3. C   (I)   (Please **calm** to my house.)
4. (C)   I   (It is hot in the **summer**.)
5. C   (I)   (He **cot** the steak with a knife.)
6. C   (I)   (What **collar** are your new shoes?)
7. (C)   I   (The story is **funny**.)
8. (C)   I   (We **won** the game.)
9. C   (I)   (Pour another **cop** of tea.)
10. C   (I)   (Please **shot** the door.)

ANSWERS TO SELF-TEST III ON PAGE 67.

1. something   wonder   ugly   (open)
2. trouble   come   (locker)   once
3. color   cups   dozen   (collar)
4. peanut   muddy   (modern)   bunny
5. (stood)   stuff   stump   stuck

172

6.	lucky	brother	just	(lock)
7.	Monday	month	(Tuesday)	Sunday
8.	(comb)	coming	cutting	country
9.	cover	(over)	oven	other
10.	rust	must	(rot)	nothing

ANSWERS TO SELF-TEST IV ON PAGE 68.

GUS: Hi *Russ!* How's my *fun loving buddy*?

RUSSELL: Very worried. I just had a run of tough luck.

GUS: Why, what's up?

RUSSELL: My bus got stuck in the mud and I lost some money. I should carry something for luck!

GUS: Yes. Here's some other advice. Never walk under ladders, and run from black cats. They're nothing but trouble!

RUSSELL: Oh, Gus. You must be a nut! Do you really believe such "mumbo jumbo"?

GUS: Don't make fun, Russ. Such customs come from many countries. You must know others!

RUSSELL: Well, the number 13 is unlucky. And, a blister on the tongue means someone is lying!

GUS: Right! But— you can have good luck too. Discover a four-leaf clover, or find bubbles in your coffee cup and you'll get a sum of money.

RUSSELL: OK, Gus. Maybe I'll have some luck this month. *Knock on wood!!!*

ANSWERS TO SELF-TEST I ON PAGE 73.

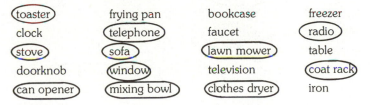

(toaster)	frying pan	bookcase	freezer
clock	(telephone)	faucet	(radio)
(stove)	(sofa)	(lawn mower)	table
doorknob	(window)	television	(coat rack)
(can opener)	(mixing bowl)	(clothes dryer)	iron

ANSWERS TO SELF-TEST II ON PAGE 73.

1. same (different) (I have a **cut**. I have a **coat**.)
2. (same) different (Row the **boat**. Row the **boat**.)
3. same (different) (The word is **hole**. The word is **hull**.)
4. (same) different (Let's go **home**. Let's go **home**.)
5. (same) different (Who **stole** it? Who **stole** it?)
6. same (different) (I see the **clothes**. I see the **claws**.)
7. same (different) (Don't **suck** that. Don't **soak** that.)

173

8. (same) different   (I have a **comb**. I have a **comb**.)
9. same (different)   (Is it **toast**? Is it **tossed**?)
10. same (different)   (He has a **loan**. He has a **lawn**.)

ANSWERS TO SELF-TEST III ON PAGE 74.

1. brown	towel	(known)	crowd
2. trouble	(notice)	normal	pocket
3. orange	carrot	(yellow)	lemon
4. foot	(toes)	ankle	eyebrow
5. politics	office	(vote)	governor
6. (comb)	tomb	bomb	come
7. essay	(poem)	story	book
8. prove	love	(stove)	shove
9. world	town	country	(road)
10. (tomato)	olive	corn	onion

ANSWERS TO SELF-TEST IV ON PAGE 74.

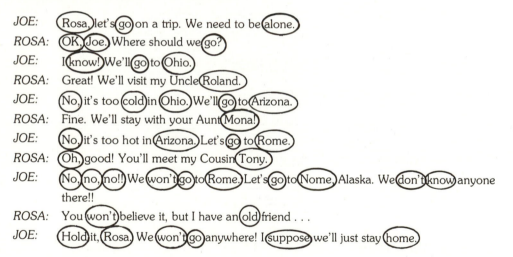

JOE: (Rosa,) let's (go) on a trip. We need to be (alone.)
ROSA: (OK, Joe.) Where should we (go?)
JOE: I (know!) We'll (go) to (Ohio.)
ROSA: Great! We'll visit my Uncle (Roland.)
JOE: (No,) it's too (cold) in (Ohio.) We'll (go) to (Arizona.)
ROSA: Fine. We'll stay with your Aunt (Mona!)
JOE: (No,) it's too hot in (Arizona.) Let's (go) to (Rome.)
ROSA: (Oh,) good! You'll meet my Cousin (Tony.)
JOE: (No, no, no!!) We (won't) (go) to (Rome.) Let's (go) to (Nome,) Alaska. We (don't) (know) anyone there!!
ROSA: You (won't) believe it, but I have an (old) friend . . .
JOE: (Hold) it, (Rosa.) We (won't) (go) anywhere! I (suppose) we'll just stay (home.)

ANSWERS TO SELF-TEST I ON PAGE 79.

1. (1) 2   (It's in the **hall**. It's in the **hull**.)
2. 1 (2)   (I dropped the **bowl**. I dropped the **ball**.)
3. (1) 2   (I said **talk**. I said **tuck**.)
4. 1 (2)   (The **stock** is high. The **stalk** is high.)
5. (1) 2   (He **sawed** it. He **sewed** it.)

174

ANSWERS TO SELF-TEST II ON PAGE 79.

AUDREY: Hi, **Paula.** Did you hear the *awful* news? Maude called off her wedding to Claude!

PAULA: Why, Audrey? I thought they were getting married in August.

AUDREY: Maude kept stalling and decided Claude was the wrong man.

PAULA: Poor Claude. He must be a lost soul.

AUDREY: Oh no. He's abroad in Austria having a ball!

PAULA: I almost forgot. What about the long tablecloth we bought them?

AUDREY: I already brought it back. The cost of the cloth will cover the cost of our lunch today.

PAULA: Audrey, you're always so thoughtful!

ANSWERS TO SELF-TEST III ON PAGE 80.

1. Ⓒ   I   (I take long **walks**.)
2. C   Ⓘ   (Who was the **collar** on the phone?)
3. Ⓒ   I   (The **store** will open at four.)
4. C   Ⓘ   (Cats and **dugs** make good pets.)
5. C   Ⓘ   (My wife loves to **tock** on the phone.)
6. C   Ⓘ   (I **boat** a new hat.)
7. C   Ⓘ   (My son likes to play foot**bowl**.)
8. Ⓒ   I   (He ate a **small** piece of pie.)
9. C   Ⓘ   (The fisherman **coat** ten snappers.)
10. Ⓒ   I   (Please **call** me tomorrow.)

ANSWERS TO REVIEW TEST I ON PAGE 83.

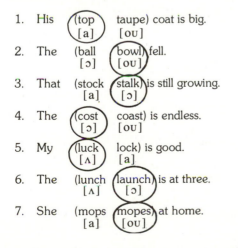

1. His   (top   taupe) coat is big.
          [a]   [ou]

2. The   (ball   bowl) fell.
          [ɔ]   [ou]

3. That (stock   stalk) is still growing.
          [a]   [ɔ]

4. The   (cost   coast) is endless.
          [ɔ]   [ou]

5. My   (luck   lock) is good.
          [ʌ]   [a]

6. The   (lunch   launch) is at three.
          [ʌ]   [ɔ]

7. She   (mops   mopes) at home.
          [a]   [ou]

175

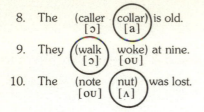

8. The (caller (collar) is old.
   [ɔ]   [a]

9. They ((walk woke) at nine.
   [ɔ]   [ou]

10. The (note nut) was lost.
   [ou] [ʌ]

ANSWERS TO REVIEW TEST II ON PAGE 84.

    [1]   [4]   [2]
1. *Does* your *father* like to *doze*?
    [2] [2]   [3]
2. A *rolling sto*ne gathers no *moss*.
    [3]   [3]   [2]
3. *Paul* sang the *song* as a *solo*.
    [4]   [1] [2]
4. *Calm* down and *come* home.
    [3] [1]   [2]   [3]
5. The *dog dug* a *hole* in the *lawn*.

ANSWERS TO REVIEW TEST III ON PAGE 85.

1. (ʌ]) [ou] [ɔ] [a] (come   fun   us)
2. [ʌ] [ou] [ɔ] ([a]) (shop   watch   pot)
3. [ʌ] [ou] ([ɔ]) [a] (lost   shore   fall)
4. [ʌ] ([ou]) [ɔ] [a] (blown   close   sold)
5. [ʌ] [ou] [ɔ] ([a]) (John   Bob   Tom)
6. (ʌ]) [ou] [ɔ] [a] (brother uncle cousin)
7. [ʌ] [ou] ([ɔ]) [a] (cause   flaw   moth)
8. [ʌ] ([ou]) [ɔ] [a] (bowl   soak   hold)
9. [ʌ] [ou] ([ɔ]) [a] (cross   fault more)
10. (ʌ]) [ou] [ɔ] [a] (Monday Sunday month)

ANSWERS TO REVIEW TEST IV ON PAGE 85.

        [ʌ]   [ʌ]
A Man *From* Kentucky

        [ʌ]   [ʌ]
A man from *Kentucky* named *Bud*

      [ʌ]   [ʌ] [ʌ]   [ʌ]
Had a *lucky young son* named *Jud*

                [ɔ]
When he bet on a *horse*

         [ɔ]   [ɔ]
It never *lost*, of *course*

    [ʌ]   [ʌ]   [ʌ]
But *one* day it got *stuck* in the *mud!*

. . . .

[a] [a]　　　[a]　　　　[a]
Tom's father was a *farmer* named *Bob*

[a]　　　　　[a]　　[a]
Who *got* very confused *on* the *job*

[ʌ]
Among his misdeeds

[ʌ]
Was mixing *some* seeds

[a]　　　　　[ɔ]　　　[a]
His *squash* tasted like *corn* on the *cob!*

. . . .

[ou]　[ou]　　[ou]
When *Moe* is *home* all *alone*

[ou]　　　　　[ou]
He just *won't* answer the *phone*

[ɔ]　　[ɔ]
It rings *all* day *long*

[ɔ]　　　[ɔ]
From *morning* till *dawn*

[ʌ]　　　[ou]　　[ou]
It's no *wonder* that *Moe* is *unknown!*

. . . .

ANSWERS TO SELF-TEST I ON PAGE 89.

1. The **girl** wore a **purple** <u>skirt</u> .
2. The **Germans** bake good <u>desserts</u> .
3. At Thanksgiving we **serve** <u>turkey</u> .
4. People **worship** in a <u>church</u> .
5. I **heard** the **chirping** of the <u>bird</u> .
6. Another **word** for handbag is <u>purse</u> .
7. A **permanent** makes your hair <u>curly</u> .
8. I **prefer** the scent of that <u>perfume</u> .
9. You should **learn** your nouns and <u>verbs</u> .
10. A **person** collects unemployment when he is out of <u>work</u> .

ANSWERS TO SELF-TEST I ON PAGE 91.

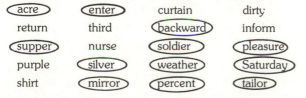

(acre)	(enter)	curtain	dirty
return	third	(backward)	inform
(supper)	nurse	(soldier)	(pleasure)
purple	(silver)	(weather)	(Saturday)
shirt	(mirror)	(percent)	(tailor)

ANSWERS TO SELF-TEST I ON PAGE 93.

1. learn   (ɝ) [ɚ]
2. sugar   [ɝ] (ɚ)
3. picture   [ɝ] (ɚ)
4. thirsty   (ɝ) [ɚ]
5. certain   (ɝ) [ɚ]

6. deliver   [ɝ] (ɚ)
7. circus   (ɝ) [ɚ]
8. world   (ɝ) [ɚ]
9. purse   (ɝ) [ɚ]
10. urgent   (ɝ) [ɚ]

ANSWERS TO SELF-TEST II ON PAGE 93.

. . . .

PEARLS

The **pearl** is one of the most (treasured) gems. Pearls are formed inside the shells of (oysters.) The largest pearl (fisheries) are in Asia. (Cultured) pearls were developed by the Chinese in the twentieth (century.) They are (larger) than (nature's) pearls. A perfect pearl that is round and has great (luster) is worth a lot of money. (Perhaps) a "diamond is a girl's best friend," but pearls will always win a woman's (favor!)

. . . .

ANSWERS TO SELF-TEST I ON PAGE 96.

1. a l p h (a) b e t
2. u t (i) l i z e
3. d (e) p e n d i n g
4. p h o t (o) g r a p h
5. p a p (a)

6. p r (e) v e n t
7. i m (i) t a t e
8. b r e a k f (a) s t
9. c (o) n t r o l
10. (a) l a r m

ANSWERS TO SELF-TEST II ON PAGE 97.

1.	about	oven	(create)	olive
2.	minute	second	seven	(leaving)
3.	(attic)	attend	allow	annoy
4.	(something)	support	supply	suppose
5.	combine	complete	(camper)	compare
6.	Canada	Georgia	Tennessee	(Wyoming)
7.	lavender	maroon	(yellow)	orange
8.	(strawberry)	banana	vanilla	chocolate
9.	lettuce	tomato	carrot	(cucumber)
10.	giraffe	zebra	(monkey)	camel

178

ANSWERS TO SELF-TEST III ON PAGE 97.

1. f a v o r i t e
2. p r i n c i p a l
3. a s s i s t a n c e
4. m e d i c a l
5. a t t e n d a n c e

6. e v i d e n c e
7. o f f e n d e d
8. d i p l o m a
9. a p a r t m e n t
10. C a n a d a

ANSWERS TO SELF-TEST I ON PAGE 101.

1. brown	down	flow	frown
2. foul	group	shout	loud
3. know	how	now	cow
4. sour	hour	tour	our
5. could	count	crown	crowd
6. thought	plough	drought	thousand
7. ounce	out	own	ouch
8. flounder	flood	flour	pounce
9. allow	about	power	arose
10. noun	consonant	vowel	sound

ANSWERS TO SELF-TEST II ON PAGE 102.

. . . .

MR. BROWN: You look out of sorts. How come?

MRS. BROWN: I'm tired out. Didn't you hear the loud noise outside all night?

MR. BROWN: I didn't hear a sound. I was "out like a light!"

MRS. BROWN: Our neighbors had a big crowd; they were shouting and howling!

MR. BROWN: Why didn't you tell them to stop clowning around?

MRS. BROWN: I didn't want to sound like a grouch.

MR. BROWN: Next time I'll go out. I'm not afraid to open my mouth!

MRS. BROWN: I knew I could count on you. Here comes our noisy neighbor Mr. Crowley, right now.

MR. BROWN: That 300 pound "powerhouse"! Sorry dear, I have to go downtown, NOW!!

MRS. BROWN: Come back, you coward!!!

. . . .

ANSWERS TO SELF-TEST I ON PAGE 105.

1.	price	crime	(pity)	pile
2.	mind	kind	(spinning)	finding
3.	sign	high	fright	(freight)
4.	(list)	cite	aisle	cried
5.	(gyp)	bye	cry	reply
6.	(niece)	nice	knife	night
7.	style	(failed)	filed	fire
8.	(pretty)	try	resign	goodbye
9.	ice cream	eye	(aim)	aisle
10.	flight	fine	(duty)	dying

ANSWERS TO SELF-TEST II ON PAGE 106.

. . . .

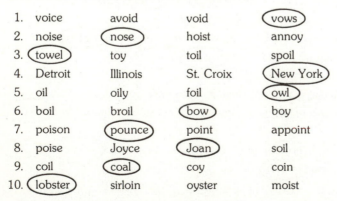

MIKE: Hi, (Myra)! It's (nice) to see you.

MYRA: (Likewise, Mike.) How are you?

MIKE: (I'm tired.) (I) just came in on a (night flight) from (Ireland.)

MYRA: What (time) did your (flight) (arrive?)

MIKE: (I arrived) at (five forty-five) in the morning.

MYRA: (I'm surprised) the (airlines) have a late (night flight.)

MIKE: If you don't (mind,) (Myra,) (I) think (I'll) go home and rest for a (while.) (I'm) really ("wiped) out!"

MYRA: It's (quite) (all right.) (Goodbye,) (Mike!)

. . . .

ANSWERS TO SELF-TEST I ON PAGE 109.

1.	voice	avoid	void	(vows)
2.	noise	(nose)	hoist	annoy
3.	(towel)	toy	toil	spoil
4.	Detroit	Illinois	St. Croix	(New York)
5.	oil	oily	foil	(owl)
6.	boil	broil	(bow)	boy
7.	poison	(pounce)	point	appoint
8.	poise	Joyce	(Joan)	soil
9.	coil	(coal)	coy	coin
10.	(lobster)	sirloin	oyster	moist

180

ANSWERS TO SELF-TEST II ON PAGE 109.

MRS. ROYCE: Hi, Mr. Lloyd. Can I help you?

MR. LLOYD: Yes, Mrs. Royce, I'd like a toy for my son Floyd.

MRS. ROYCE: We have quite a choice of toys. What about a firetruck?

MR. LLOYD: That's too noisy. Besides, my boy would destroy it!

MRS. ROYCE: Here's a paint and oil set.

MR. LLOYD: That's messy. His mother will be annoyed if he soils anything.

MRS. ROYCE: Let me point out this electric train.

MR. LLOYD: Wow! I never had a toy like that as a boy!

MRS. ROYCE: Your boy will enjoy it. Mr. Lloyd? Please turn off the set. Mr. Lloyd, you can't hear my voice!!

MR. LLOYD: Did you say something, Mrs. Royce? I'm playing with Floyd's new toy!

MRS. ROYCE: I guess he's made his choice. I hope he lets his boy use it once in a while!

ANSWERS TO REVIEW TEST I ON PAGE 113.

[ə] as in *UPON*	[aʊ] as in *OUT*	[aɪ] as in *I*	[ɔɪ] as in *OIL*
alone	frown	bright	join
upon	mouth	fright	destroy
lemon	sound	while	boil
open	vow	rhyme	voyage
circus	mountain	guide	loyal
humid	cloud	rely	noise

ANSWERS TO REVIEW TEST II ON PAGE 114.

   3   1   3   2   3   2   1   1
Fried chicken is liked throughout the United States. However, it is considered a famous dish
               2   4
from the South. Here is the recipe for you to enjoy.

      1
Ingredients:
   3   2   2
One frying chicken (about three or four pounds)
       2
One cup of flour
  2   4
Eight ounces of oil

Combine flour with seasonings of your own choice. Roll chicken in flour and coat on all sides. Pour oil into large-sized frying pan. Heat oil until very hot (almost boiling). Fry three or four pieces at a time including breasts, wings and thighs. Cover tightly and cook for around twenty-five minutes. Allow chicken to steam. Remove cover and cook for nine or ten more minutes until pieces are completely browned. Take chicken out of pan and dry on paper towel.

ANSWERS TO GENERAL REVIEW ACTIVITY I ON PAGE 117.

[i]	[ɪ]	[eɪ]	[ɛ]	[æ]	[a]	[u]
be	in	they	many	and	are	to
he	it	make	when	that	not	do
we	is	there	very	have	on	you
people	this	take	them	an	want	two
these	if	their	well	as		school
she	will	state	then	at		who
see	with	way	any	man		too
each	which	great		can		
	his	day		has		
	thing	may		than		
	think					
	been					
	give					

[ʊ]	[ʌ]	[oʊ]	[ɔ]	[ɝ]	[aɪ]	[aʊ]
would	the	so	for	work	I	out
could	of	know	or	her	light	our
should	a	only	all	were	by	about
	one	most	more	person	time	
	was		because	first	my	
	but		course		like	
	some		also			
	much					
	other					
	from					
	what					
	up					
	just					

182

ANSWERS TO GENERAL REVIEW ACTIVITY II ON PAGE 118.

1. ([ɛ]) [ɪ] [i] (head   fence   rest)
2. [ɛ] ([ɪ]) [i] (since   knit   kick)
3. [eɪ] ([a]) [æ] (lock   hot   mark)
4. ([eɪ]) [a] [æ] (place   break   tame)
5. [u] [ʊ] ([ʌ]) (once   luck   some)
6. ([u]) [ʊ] [ʌ] (lose   blue   soon)
7. ([aɪ]) [ɔ] [oʊ] (white   dime   knife)
8. [aɪ] ([ɔ]) [oʊ] (fall   walk   taught)
9. ([aʊ]) [ɔɪ] [ɝ] (loud   now   mouth)
10. [aʊ] [ɔɪ] ([ɝ]) (first   burn   word)

ANSWERS TO GENERAL REVIEW ACTIVITY II ON PAGE 119.

1. ([ʌ]) [oʊ] [ɔ]   us   country subject women   come
2. [ɔ]   ([eɪ]) [æ]   play   change   back   made   raise
3. ([i]) [ɪ] [ɛ]   mean   speech   teacher need   subject
4. [a]   ([æ]) [eɪ]   example back   after   rather   part
5. [æ]   [eɪ] ([ɛ])   help   less   second   number   said
6. ([a]) [oʊ] [ɔ]   large   job   home   top   college
7. [i]   ([ɪ]) [aɪ]   quite   him   picture into   little
8. ([aɪ]) [eɪ] [aʊ]   might   why   high   life   say
9. [aɪ] ([aʊ]) [ɔɪ]   down   around   how   those   now
10. ([ɔ]) [a] [oʊ]   before   small   long   old   cost

ANSWERS TO GENERAL REVIEW ACTIVITY II ON PAGE 120.

1. [ɛ] The kids were **FED** and put to **B**ED.
2. [aɪ] The shining **LIGHT** was very **BR**IGHT.
3. [aʊ] We heard the crowd **SHOUT** as the batter struck **O**UT.
4. [oʊ] My friend **ROSE** wears pretty **CL**OTHES.
5. [eɪ] Kate made a **DATE**; don't be **L**ATE.
6. [a] After **DARK** the dogs start to **B**ARK.
7. [u] It's too **COOL** in the swimming **P**OOL.
8. [ɔɪ] Roy gave my **BOY** a brand new **T**OY.
9. [ʊ] Be sure to **LOOK** in the phone **B**OOK.
10. [æ] Why does **DAD** look unhappy and **S**AD?

183

[ɪ]   [ɔɪ]

TREES was written by Joyce Kilmer.   [ɪ] [i] [ɔɪ]

[ɪ]   [ɛ] [i]

I think that I shall never see   [ɪ] [i] [ɛ]

[ʌ]   [ə] [i]

A poem as lovely as a tree   [ʌ] [i] [ə]

[u]   [aʊ]

A tree whose hungry mouth is prest   [u] [oʊ] [aʊ]

[ɛ]   [ɝ]   [ɛ]

Against the earth's sweet flowing breast; [ɛ] [ɝ] [ɛ]

[ʊ]   [a] [ɔ]

A tree that looks at God all day,   [a] [ɔ] [ʊ]

[ɪ]   [a]   [eɪ]

And lifts her leafy arms to pray;   [a] [eɪ] [ɪ]

[æ]   [ɝ]

A tree that may in summer wear   [æ] [ɝ] [a]

[ɛ]   [a]

A nest of robins in her hair;   [a] [eɪ] [ɛ]

[ə]   [oʊ]   [eɪ]

Upon whose bosom snow has lain   [ə] [eɪ] [oʊ]

[ɪ]   [eɪ]

Who intimately lives with rain.   [u] [eɪ] [ɪ]

[eɪ]   [u]

Poems are made by fools like me   [u] [eɪ] [aɪ]

[oʊ]   [i]

But only God can make a tree.   [i] [oʊ] [a]

ANSWERS TO SELF-TEST I ON PAGE 127.

1. themselves   them (selves)
2. birthday   (birth) day
3. engineer   en gi (neer)
4. September   Sep (tem) ber
5. Saturday   (Sat) ur day

ANSWERS TO SELF-TEST II ON PAGE 128.

1. (agent)   annoy   allow   agree
2. upon   until   undo   (under)

184

3. (protect)   program   pronoun   protein

4. token   toaster   (today)   total

5. supper   sunken   suffer   (support)

6. explain   (extra)   excite   exam

7. (deepen)   deny   devote   degree

8. (repair)   reason   recent   reader

9. invite   invent   inform   (instant)

10. open   (oppose)   over   only

ANSWERS TO SELF-TEST III ON PAGE 128.

1. Keep a ①2 *record* of your expenses.

2. The police don't 1 ② *suspect* anyone.

3. The student will 1② *present* a speech.

4. The ①2 *present* was not wrapped.

5. The ① 2 3 *invalid* was in the hospital.

ANSWERS TO SELF-TEST IV ON PAGE 129.

① ②   ① 2   ① 2
MONEY by Richard Armour

① 2
Workers earn it,

①   2
Spendthrifts burn it,

① 2
Bankers lend it,

① 2
Women spend it,

① 2
Forgers fake it,

① 2
Taxes take it,

①2
Dying leave it

1 ②
Heirs receive it,

(1) 2
Thrifty save it,

(1)2
Misers crave it,

(1) 2
Robbers seize it,

    1   (2)
Rich increase it,

(1)   2
Gamblers lose it. . . .

I could use it!

ANSWERS TO SELF-TEST I ON PAGE 135.

1. (Mary) is a (good) (friend.)
2. (Steve) is (tall) and (handsome.)
3. It's (early) in the (morning.)
4. The (baby) (caught) a (cold.)
5. I (ate) a (piece) of (pie.)
6. The (store) (opens) at (nine.)
7. My (shoes) (hurt) my (feet.)
8. (Please) (look) for the (book.)
9. He's (leaving) in a (week.)
10. We (walked) in the (snow.)

ANSWERS TO SELF-TEST II ON PAGE 135.

1. black **bird**   (**black**bird)
2. copper **head**   (**copper**head)
3. (blue **bell**)   **blue**bell
4. light **house**   (**light**house)
5. (white **house**)   **White** House

6. (cheap **skates**)   **cheap**skates
7. (white **fish**)   **white**fish
8. blue **bird**   (**blue**bird)
9. (black **board**)   **black**board
10. green **house**   (**green**house)

ANSWERS TO SELF-TEST III ON PAGE 136.

1. Mary wants a cup of coffee.
2. The show started at eight.
3. The movie was very funny.
4. Sue ate a slice of cake.
5. We met a couple of friends of mine.

186

ANSWERS TO SELF-TEST IV ON PAGE 136.

1. Mary is Anna's (friend.) (She isn't her cousin).
2. Juan is (married) to Anna. (They aren't engaged anymore.)
3. She's from Washington, (D.C.) (She's not from Washington state.)
4. She lives in the white (house.) (She doesn't live in the White House.)
5. Her house is on First (Street.) (It isn't on First Avenue.)
6. Anna and Juan got married (three) years ago. (Not five years ago.)
7. They (own) a small home. (They don't rent.)
8. Mary wants to come in a (week.) (She doesn't want to wait a month.)
9. She'll bring her (collie) and snakes. (She's not bringing her poodle.)
10. Mary is opening a (pet) store. (Not a toy store.)

ANSWERS TO SELF-TEST I ON PAGE 141.

1. I'm a student. (I am)
2. Lynn doesn't play tennis. (does not)
3. We've seen that movie. (We have)
4. You're quite right. (You are)
5. His brother can't come. (cannot)

ANSWERS TO SELF-TEST II on page 141.

1. Meet me at the bus stop // after you're done.
   Meet me at the bus // stop after you're done.
2. Bill Brown the mayor will // speak tonight.
   Bill Brown // the mayor // will speak tonight.
3. Please clean your room // before leaving.
   Please clean your // room before leaving.
4. The truth is I don't // like it.
   The truth is // I don't like it.
5. Cervantes // the famous author // wrote Don Quixote.
   Cervantes the famous author wrote // Don Quixote.

187

Reduced Form	Full Form
Howarya?	How are you?
It's	It is
Doyawanna	Do you want to
cup ə coffee	cup of coffee
That's	That is
I'm	I am
gonna	going to
don't	do not
t ə th ə movies	to the movies
won't	will not
He's	He is
We'll	We will
meetchə	meet you
haftə	have to
It's	It has
Frannie's	Frannie is
hastə	has to

FRANCES BLACK: Hello, this is the Black residence. This is Frances Black speaking.

ELLIE WHITE: (Howarya) Frannie. (It's) Ellie. (Doyawanna) come over for a (cup ə coffee?)

FRANCES BLACK: Elinor, I am very sorry. I cannot visit you. I am going to lunch at the Club.

ELLIE WHITE: (That's) OK. I'm (gonna) eat at Burger Palace. Why (don't) we go (t ə th ə movies) tonight?

FRANCES BLACK: We will not be able to join you. We have tickets for the opera.

ELLIE WHITE: My husband Sam (won't) like that. (He's) more of a wrestling fan. We'll (meetchə) some other night.

FRANCES BLACK: Elinor, I really have to go now. It has been most pleasant speaking with you.

ELLIE WHITE: I (haftə) go now too. It's been great talking to you. (Hangs up the phone) (Frannie's) a nice girl, but she (hastə) learn to relax!

188

ANSWERS TO SELF-TEST I ON PAGE 149.

1. (Ron did 90 sit-ups.)   Ron did 90 sit-ups.
2. It only cost ten cents.   (It only cost ten cents.)
3. (He's really smart.)   He's really smart.
4. (She's been married eight times.)   She's been married eight times.
5. You drank two gallons of wine. (You drank two gallons of wine.)
6. (The bridge is three miles high.)   The bridge is three miles high.
7. (Sue has good taste.)   Sue has good taste.
8. They ate pickles with milk.   (They ate pickles with milk.)
9. He read the book in an hour.   (He read the book in an hour.)
10. (You baked a cake.)   You baked a cake.

ANSWERS TO SELF-TEST II ON PAGE 149

1. When's your birthday?   ↘
2. Did you see my friend?   ↗
3. How are you?   ↘
4. I'm fine, thank you.   ↘
5. Why were you absent?   ↘

ANSWERS TO SELF-TEST III ON PAGE 150

HUSBAND: Hi, honey. ↘ What did you do today? ↘

WIFE: I went shopping. ↘

HUSBAND: You went shopping? ↗ Again? ↗

WIFE: Yes. ↘ The store had a big sale. ↘ Everything was half price. ↘

HUSBAND: What did you buy now? ↘

WIFE: I bought this blouse for thirty dollars. ↘ Isn't it stunning? ↗

HUSBAND: Yes, it's stunning. ↘ I'm the one that's stunned. ↘

WIFE: Do you like the green hat ___ or the red one? ↘

HUSBAND: I like the cheaper one. ↘

WIFE: I also bought a belt, → scarf, → dress, → and shoes. ↘

HUSBAND: Stop it! ↘ I'm afraid to hear any more. ↘ Do we have any money left? ↗

WIFE: Yes dear, we have lots of money left. ↘ I saved two hundred dollars on my
          new clothes, → so I bought you a set of golf clubs. ↘

HUSBAND: Really? ↗ I always said you were a great shopper! ↘

****

SPANISH STUDY GUIDE

****

AL ESTUDIANTE

Usted compró este programa porque sentía una necesidad de mejorar su pronunciación de inglés como segundo idioma. Sabemos que es muy frustrante que nos digan: ''No puedo entenderle por su acento.'' También, sabemos el miedo que usted puede sentir al decir ciertas palabras y ser malentendido. Muchos de nuestros estudiantes tienen miedo de pronunciar palabras tales como: ''sheet'' y ''beach.'' En su lugar usan ''piece'' y ''ocean.'' Así que entendemos como usted se siente y queremos ayudarle. Así que, ¡no se preocupe. Ni deje de usar ciertas palabras o frases por temor a ser malentendido!

Este libro ha sido escrito para USTED. Muy pronto usted descubrirá que este programa ha sido diseñado para ayudarle a superar sus problemas de pronunciación al hablar inglés. Este es un programa independiente que usted podrá utilizar por su cuenta. El manual ha sido escrito con términos sencillos y fáciles de entender. Es acompañado de cintas magnetofónicas para ayudarle en la pronunciación de vocales del inglés-americano. Usted no necesita una maestra (o terapista del hable) para usar este programa.

El manual contiene varios capítulos cubriendo las vocales y diptongos del idioma inglés. A cada capítulo le sigue un formato que contiene las siguientes secciones:

Pronunciando el Sonido

En esta sección se da una explicación sencilla de como se pronuncia el sonido. Se dan detalles de la posición de los articuladores (labios, lengua, etc.).

Palabras Claves en Español

En esta sección, se dan palabras claves en español que contienen en la vocal equivalente en inglés. Así se le dará un sonido familiar que usted puede asociar.

Posibles Problemas de Pronunciación para Personas de Habla Hispana

En esta sección se le explica porqué la pronunciación de las vocales en inglés son problemáticas para usted y cómo estas difieren de la pronunciación de las vocales en español.

190

Sugerencias

Esta sección contiene una serie de reglas que le ayudarán a pronunciar el sonido. Han sido diseñadas para ayudarle a usar los patrones de deletreo como guía de pronunciación.

Ejercicios

Esta sección consiste de una serie de ejercicios diseñados para darle práctica con los sonidos de las vocales tal y como ocurren en las palabras, frases comunes y oraciones.

Exámenes

Esta sección incluye una variedad de exámenes breves diseñados para que usted se dé cuenta del progreso que ha tenido. Se examinará su capacidad para reconocer y pronunciar el sonido en palabras, oraciones y conversación.

Para un "Encore". . . . .

Esta sección ha sido diseñada con el propósito de que usted use la vocal clave en situaciones del diario vivir. Una serie de actividades de escuchar, lectura y conversación se incluyen al final de cada capítulo.

Los capítulos adicionales incluyen explicaciones y ejercicios para los patrones de fuerza, ritmo y entonación en el idioma inglés. Las respuestas correctas se encontrarán en el apéndice.

Las cintas magnetofónicas que acompañan el manual contienen secciones de cada capítulo (están claramente marcadas en el manual) y han sido diseñadas para proveer un modelo correcto de pronunciación para cada sonido. Favor de referirse a la página v para un esquema del material que se incluye en las cintas.

Como Usar el Programa

Ahora usted está listo para comenzar el programa. Los únicos materiales que necesitará serán: una grabadora para las cintas y un espejo que le ayude a colocar los articuladores al hacer un sonido. Busque un lugar tranquilo y cómodo donde practicar: Llénese de entusiasmo y determinación de que mejorará su pronunciación—¡y usted estará listo para empezar!!

Antes de comenzar el programa, lea el capítulo 1 en el manual y toque la cinta 1 (lado A) para familiarizarse con el formato de las lecciones. (Asegúrese que entiende las explicaciones en el manual antes de empezar las prácticas orales).

Ejercicios

Renueve la marcha de la cinta al comienzo y mire el ejercicio A, capítulo 1 (página 12). Practique el ejercicio como le indican las direcciones. Repita las palabras después del instructor, durante las pausas. Usted puede parar la cinta cuando usted desee repetir una sección. Si usted tiene dificultad en algún momento, pare la cinta, y repase las instrucciones de pronunciación de la vocal. Revise el espejo y asegúrese que sus articuladores están en la posición correcta. Continue de esta misma manera con cada ejercicio hasta que usted esté seguro de que puede decir las palabras y oraciones con facilidad. Antes de comenzar la próxima sección, repita el material despues del instructor sin mirar el libro.

Exámenes

Una vez que se sienta seguro de que puede hacer los ejercicios, comienze con las pruebas o exámenes. Las instrucciones para cada exámen varían: así que, lea cada una de ellas cuidadosamente antes de empezar. Al terminar cada exámen, apague la grabadora y revise las respuestas en el apéndice. Si usted tiene alguna dificultad con los exámenes, regrese al principio del capítulo y repita los ejercicios. Las actividades de más dificultad son los diálogos y los párrafos, repáselos varias veces a medida que va progresando en el manual.

Para un "Encore". . . . .

Cuando se sienta satisfecho con su pronunciación de la vocal específica, usted está listo para pasar del libro a las situaciones del diario vivir. Estas son sugerencias para automatizar el proceso de pronunciación. Trate de buscar otras maneras de incorporar el sonido aprendido a su rutina diaria.

Repaso de Capítulos

El repaso de capítulos ha sido diseñado para darle a usted práctica adicional. Termine los exámenes como hizo en los capítulos anteriores. Si tiene problema con algunas de las vocales, regrese al capítulo y repáselo.

Sesiones de Práctica

Es muy importante practicar. Trate de hacer una rutina de el tiempo dedicado a estos estudios. Lo ideal es practicar diariamente, pero si su tiempo es corto, practique por lo menos de 3 a 4 veces a la semana (por 20—30 minutos). Sabemos que leer un libro y oir cintas es un trabajo muy ardúo y difícil. Tómese un descanso cuando se sienta cansado. Continue su sesión de estudio cuando se sienta fresco y descansado. ¡NO TRATE DE HACERLO TODO DE UNA VEZ! *El perfeccionamiento toma tiempo. Pero poco a poco llegará legos!*

Mantenga la grabadora y las cintas cerca de su area de trabajo, ya sea en la cocina o en el auto. Lo importante es practicar cuando se sienta relajado, descansado y motivado, así, lo hará lo mejor posible sin mucho esfuerzo. *¡RECUERDE, QUE LA PRÁCTICA ES LO QUE NOS LLEVA A LA PERFECCIÓN! ! !*

Otras Maneras de Mejorar su Pronunciación

Escuchar es una manera de mejorar la pronunciación. Aproveche el mayor número de oportunidades para escuchar hablar inglés. Puede hacerlo siguiendo estas sugerencias:

1. Mire las noticias en la televisión. Preste atención a la pronunciación del locutor. Repita algunas de las palabras o frases que el dice en voz alta. (*No se preocupe, su familia no pensará que está hablando solo! Le admirarán pues saben que usted esta tratando de mejorarse.*)

2. Oiga las noticias en la radio de 5 a 10 minutos. Repita algunas de las palabras o frases del locutor. (*Si las personas le miran mal porque creen que usted está loco, dígale que está practicando su pronunciación!*)

3. Cuando su programa de televisión favorito comienze, trate de entender el diálogo sin mirar a la pantalla. *Pero,* si tiene que mirar la pantalla para entenderlo, entonces espere los comerciales para practicar la destreza de escuchar.

4. Converse frecuentemente con alguien nativo del idioma inglés-americano.

5. Pregúntele al que le está escuchando si su pronunciación ha sido correcta. *Ellos se sentirán felices de poderle ayudar!*

6. **Pero lo mas importante de todo—SEA VALIENTE!** Los ejercicios están repletos de expresiones comunes. Use algunas de ellas en su conversación diaria y así nadie se dará cuenta de que está haciendo su tarea!!

Aunque este programa tiene come énfasis la pronunciación, el material incluido en el manual es de gran ayuda para su vocabulario. Cuando no entienda una frase o expresión idiomática, búsquela en el diccionario. Escriba la definición en el maual y así no se le olvidará.

Usted se preguntará cuanto tiempo le tomará para notar una mejoría. Nosotros creemos que el curso provee todo lo que usted necesita para mejorar su pronunciación. Si usted sigue el programa, en el orden indicado, usted notará una mejoría en un par de semanas. *Recuerde que mientras más practique, mas rápida será su mejoría!*

La motivación es un factor que puede contribuir enormemente. Muchos actores y actrices han tenido que perder el acento para poderse convertir en artistas de cine. No le podemos garantizar un contrato en el cine, pero sí podemos garantizarle que este programa le ayudará a que sea entendido y se comunique mejor en la vida cotidiana. **¡Buena suerte!**

¡Vire la página, y vamos a comenzar!

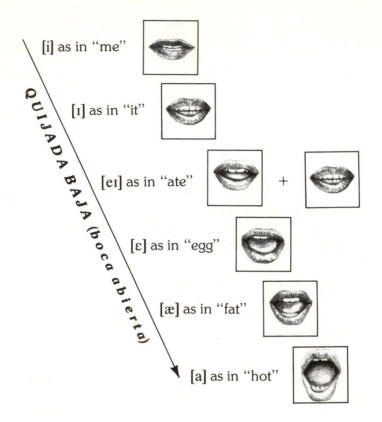

[i] as in "me"

[ɪ] as in "it"

[eɪ] as in "ate"   +

[ɛ] as in "egg"

[æ] as in "fat"

[a] as in "hot"

QUIJADA BAJA (boca abierta)

En las fotos usted puede ver como la quijada se mueve de una posición cerrada a una posición abierta durante la producción en secuencia de las vocales: [i] [ɪ] [eɪ] [ɛ] [æ] [a]. El familiarizarse con esta secuencia y el entender esta relación de una vocal a la otra le ayudará con la producción de las vocales en la sección I del manual. Ejemplos:

El símbolo fonético [ɪ] representa un sonido entre [i] y [eɪ]. Es producida con la quijada y la lengua un poco más elevadas que para la [eɪ], pero no tan elevado como para la [i].

El símbolo [æ] representa un sonido entre [ɛ] y [a]. [æ] se produce con la quijada más abierta que para la [ɛ], pero no tan abierta como para la [a].

Estas explicaciones le parecerán algo confusas al principio. Mire las ilustraciones cuando tenga dificultad con las vocales de la sección I. Repita la secuencia [i] [ɪ] [eɪ] [ɛ] [æ] [a] varias veces. Asegúrese que ve y siente la sucesión progresiva de la lengua y quijada bajando lentamente a medida que produce cada sonido.

194

PRONUNCIANDO SECCIÓN II VOCALES

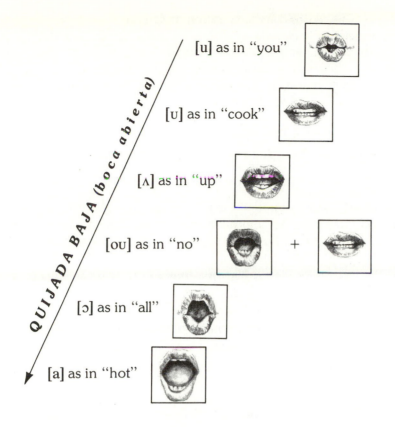

QUIJADA BAJA (boca abierta)

[u] as in "you"

[ʊ] as in "cook"

[ʌ] as in "up"

[oʊ] as in "no"   +

[ɔ] as in "all"

[a] as in "hot"

Otra vez usted puede ver como la quijada se mueve de una posición cerrada a una posición abierta al producir la secuencia de vocales. Practique pronunciando la serie varias veces. Coloque su mano debajo de la barbilla y sienta como su quijada va bajando a medida que pronuncia cada vocal.

Mire las fotos cuando se sienta confundido sobre la pronunciación de alguna de las vocales en la sección II de este libro. Repita la secuencia [u] [ʊ] [ʌ] [oʊ] [ɔ] [a] varias veces. Usted podrá ver y sentir como la quijada va bajando a medida que pronuncia las vocales en la secuencia. *Trátelo! Yi verá como funciona!*

PRONUNCIANDO [i] COMO EN "ME" (Página 11 en su libro)

LABIOS: se colocan tensos como en posición de sonrisa
MANDIBULA: completamente elevada
LENGUA: se coloca alta hacía el cielo de la boca

El sonido [i] en inglés es similar a la "i" fuerte en español. (En realidad, [i] es más larga y más prolongada que en español.)

Posibles Problemas de Pronunciación para Personas de Habla Hispana

Los problemas de pronunciación pueden ocurrir debido a los patrones confusos de pronunciación y deletreo del idioma inglés. Un ejemplo de estos es la similitud en pronunciación entre [i] y [ɪ]. Cuando usted substituye [i] por [ɪ]:

sheep *(oveja)* se convierte en **ship** *(barco)*
eat *(comer)* se convierte en **it** *(lo)*

¡No se preocupe! Usted ya conoce la [i] y como en en español. Recuerde que tiene que sentir la tension en sus labios, lengua y quijada. La [i] es un sonido largo, recuerde que tiene que p r o l o n g a r l o.

PRONUNCIANDO [ɪ] COMO EN "IT" (Página 15 en su libro)

LABIOS: están relajados y un poco abiertos
MANDIBULA: se coloca un poco mas baja que para [i]
LENGUA: está alta, pero más baja que para [i]

Posibles Problemas de Pronunciación para Personas de Habla Hispana

La vocal [ɪ] no existe en español y puede ser dificil para usted reconocerla y decirla. Probablemente usted substituya la [i] ya que le es más familiar. Cuando usted substituye [i] por [ɪ]:

hit *(golpear)* se convierte en **heat** *(calor)*
itch *(picazón)* se convierte en **each** *(cada)*

A medida que practica los ejercicios recuerde, no sonria y coloque los labios tensos como para [i]. [ɪ] es un sonido corto y rápido y los labios casi no se mueven al decirlo.

196

PRONUNCIANDO [eɪ] COMO EN "ATE" (Página 22 en su libro)

LABIOS: están abiertos y no redondos
MANDIBULA: se levanta con la lengua y ligeramente cerrada
LENGUA: se mueve de la posición media a tocar casi el cielo de la boca

[eɪ] es un diptongo. Que comienza con la [e] y termina con la [ɪ]. [eɪ] se pronuncia de la misma manera que las letras "ei" o "ey" en español.

Posibles Problemas de Pronunciación para Personas de Habla Hispana

Los problemas de pronunciación pueden ocurrir debido a los patrones confusos de pronunciación y deletreo del idioma inglés. Un ejemplo de estos es la similitud en pronunciación entre [eɪ] y [ɛ]. Cuando usted substituye [ɛ] por [eɪ]:

late	(tarde) se convierte en	*let*	(permitir)
paper	(papel) se convierte en	*pepper*	(pimiento)

PRONUNCIANDO [ɛ] COMO EN "EGG" (Página 28 en su libro)

LABIOS: levemente abiertos y no redondeados
MANDIBULA: algo mas abierta que para [eɪ]
LENGUA: punto medio en la boca

La vocal [ɛ] en inglés es similar al sonido de la letra "e" en algunas palabras en español. ([ɛ] es actualmente más corta y más ligera que la "e" en español.)

Posibles Problemas de Pronunciación para Personas de Habla Hispana

Los problemas de pronunciación ocurren al confundir patrones de deletreo del idioma inglés y debido a la similitud entre la [ɛ] y otros sonidos.

Si se reemplaza [ɛ] por [eɪ]: *pen (pluma)* sonará como *pain (dolor)*
Si se reemplaza [ɛ] por [æ]: *met (conocí)* sonará como *mat (estera)*

Al pronunciar [ɛ], abra la boca más que para [eɪ] pero menos abierta que para [æ].

PRONUNCIANDO [æ] COMO EN "AT" (Página 34 en su libro)

LABIOS: mas abiertas que para [ɛ]
MANDIBULA: muy abierta, pero menos que para [a]
LENGUA: está baja cerca del piso de la boca

Posibles Problemas de Pronunciación para Personas de Habla Hispana

La vocal [æ] no existe en español y puede ser dificil oirla y producirla. Tambien, usted puede tener la tendencia a tratar de pronunciarla como "a" en español. Ejemplos:

Si usted dice [a] en lugar de [æ]: **hat** *(sombrero)* sonará como **hot** *(caliente)*
Si usted dice [ɛ] en lugar de [æ]: **bad** *(malo)* sonará como **bed** *(cama)*

Al producir la vocal [æ], recuerde, de abrir los labios y la boca. Pero no tan grande que sienta que esta diciendo [a] en su lugar!

PRONUNCIANDO [a] COMO EN "HOT" (Página 39 en su libro)

LABIOS: completamente abiertos como en la posición de un bostezo
MANDIBULA: más abajo que para ninguna otra vocal
LENGUA: plana en el piso de la boca

El sonido [a] en inglés tiene la misma pronunciación como la fuerza "a" en español.

Posibles Problemas de Pronunciación para Personas de Habla Hispana

La razon principal por la cual tendrá problemas se deberá a los patrones irregulares de deletreo de la vocal [a]. La letra "o" en inglés se pronuncia frecuentemente como "a" en "casa" o "acá".

Si substituye [ou] por [a]: **not** *(no)*   se oirá como **note**   *(nota)*
Si substituye [ʌ] por [a]: **not** *(no)*   se oirá como **nut**   *(nuez)*
Si substituye [ɔ] por [a]: **cot** *(catre)* se oirá como **caught** *(cogió)*

Confuso ¿no? Pero no se preocupe, usted ya sabe pronunciar [a] en español.

198

PRONUNCIANDO [u] COMO EN "YOU" (Página 51 en su libro)

LABIOS: tensos como en posición para silbar
QUIJADA: completamente levantada
LENGUA: alta cerca del cielo de la boca

El sonido [u] en el inglés es similar a la "u" fuerte en español. (En realidad, [u] es algo más prolongada en español.)

Posibles Problemas de Pronunciación para Personas de Habla Hispana

Los problemas de pronunciación pueden ocurrir debido a los patrones confusos de deletreo en inglés y debido a la similitud que existe entre la [u] y la [ʊ] que describirémos más adelante. Cuando usted substituye [ʊ] por [u]:

> **pool** *(piscina)* suena como **pull** *(tirar)*
> **suit** *(traje)* suena como **soot** *(hollin)*

¡Usted puede hacerlo! Usted sabe pronunciar [u] en español. Recuerde que los labios deben permanecer tensos y en posición de silbar. El sonido de la [u] debe ser **largo**; asegúrese que lo **prolonga.**

PRONUNCIANDO [ʊ] COMO EN "COOK" (Página 55 en su libro)

LABIOS: están relajados y algo abiertos
QUIJADA: algo mas baja que para [u]
LENGUA: está alta pero algo mas baja que para [u]

Posibles Problemas de Pronunciación para Personas de Habla Hispana

La vocal [ʊ] no existe en español y puede ser dificil para usted el distinguirla y producirla. Puede que usted la substituya por la [u] que usted ya conoce. Cuando usted substituye [u] por [ʊ]:

> **full** *(lleno)* se oirá como **fool** *(tonto)*
> **cook** *(cocinero)* se oirá como **kook** *(persona alocada)*

Al decir las palabras en los ejercicios, recuerde no sacar los labios sino poner-
los tensos como en [u]. [u] es un sonido **CORTO** y **RAPIDO;** sus labios casi
no se mueven al decirla.

PRONUNCIANDO [ʌ] COMO EN "UP" (Página 62 en su libro)

LABIOS: relajados y levemente separados
QUIJADA: relajada y levemente baja
LENGUA: relajada en el medio de la boca

Posibles Problemas de Pronunciación para Personas de Habla Hispana

La vocal [ʌ] no existe en español y por eso es dificil el oírla y pronunciarla.
También se confunde facilmente debido a los patrones irregulares del idioma
inglés y es fácil substituirla por sonidos que son mas familiares para usted.
Ejemplos:

Si substituye [a] por [ʌ]:   **color** (color) sonará como **collar** (cuello)
Si substituye [ou] por [ʌ]:   **come** (venir) sonará como **comb** (peine)
Si substituye [ɔ] por [ʌ]:   **done** (hecho) sonará como **dawn** (amanecer)

Recuerde que la [ʌ] es muy corta. No debe sentir ninguna tensión al decirla y
los labios casi no se mueven al pronunciarla.

PRONUNCIANDO [ou] COMO EN "OH" (Página 69 en su libro)

LABIOS: tensos y muy redondeados
QUIJADA: levantada con la lengua y levemente cerrada
LENGUA: se deslisa de posición media al cielo de la boca

[ou] es un diptongo. Comienza con [o] y termina con [u]. [ou] en inglés es
similar al la "o" acentuada en español. ([ou] es algo más larga y prolongada
que la "o" en español.)

200

Posibles Problemas de Pronunciación para Personas de Habla Hispana

Otra vez, los problemas de pronunciación surgirán por los patrones confusos de deletreo del idioma inglés y similitud que tiene con otros sonidos. Ejemplos:

Si substituye [ʌ] por [oʊ]: ***coat*** *(abrigo)*   sonará como ***cut*** *(cortar)*
Si substituye [ɔ] por [oʊ]: ***bold*** *(valiente)*   sonará como ***bald*** *(calvo)*

Al producir el diptongo [oʊ] redondee los labios como para la letra "O"! [oʊ] es un sonido ***LARGO.*** *Prolóngelo!*

PRONUNCIANDO [ɔ] COMO EN "ALL" (Página 76 en su libro)

LABIOS: tensos en forma ovalada y ligeramente empujada hacía afuera
QUIJADA: mas abierta que para [oʊ]
LENGUA: baja en el piso de la boca

Posibles Problemas de Pronunciación para Personas de Habla Hispana

La vocal [ɔ] es otra de las "problemáticas" ya que no existe en español. Patrones confusos en deletreo hacen que la substitución sea frecuente. Ejemplos:

Si substituye [a] por [ɔ]:   ***caller*** *(llamador)*   sonará como ***collar*** *(cuello)*

Si substituye [oʊ] por [ɔ]:   ***bought*** *(compró)*   sonará como ***boat*** *(barco)*

Si substituye [ʌ] por [ɔ]:   ***bought*** *(compró)*   sonará como ***but*** *(pero)*

A medida que escuche a su maestra o al profesor en la cinta, su pronunciación mejorará. Recuerde de protuberar los labios y bajar la quijada al decir [ɔ].

PRONUNCIANDO [ɝ] COMO EN "SERVE" (Página 87 en su libro)

LABIOS: protuberantes y levemente abiertos
QUIJADA: levemente baja
LENGUA: en posición media en la boca

[ɝ] es un sonido que tan solo ocurre en sílabas accentuadas.

Posibles Problemas de Pronunciación para Personas de Habla Hispana

La vocal [ɝ] no existe en español. Sin embargo los que hablan español no tienen dificultad al pronunciarla. Tan solo recuerde que [ɝ] siempre recibe enfasis fuerte y que tan solo se encuentra en las sílabas y palabras acentuadas. Se produce con los labios levemente protuberantes y con los músculos de la lengua tensos.

PRONUNCIANDO [ɚ] COMO EN "FATHER" (Página 90 en su libro)

Es dificil oir la diferencia entre [ɚ] y [ɝ] cuando se dicen estos sonidos fuera del contexto de una palabra. Sin embargo, se produce [ɝ] con mucho meno fuerza que [ɚ]. [ɝ] tan solo se encuentra en las sílabas inacentuadas de las palabras.

Posibles Problemas de Pronunciación para Personas de Habla Hispana

La vocal [ɚ] no existe en español. La posición de los labios y de la quijada es lo mismo como para la vocal [ɝ]. Pero, se produce con los músculos de la lengua completamente relajados. [ɚ] nunca recibe enfasis fuerte y se encuentra solamente en las sílabas y palabras inacentuadas.

PRONUNCIANDO [ə] COMO EN "A" (Página 94 en su libro)

[ə] es el sonido que resulta cuando cualquier vocal en una palabra en inglés no se acentua. Las vocales no acentuadas casi siempre suenan como [ə]. Cualquier letra o combinación de letras pueden representar "*schwa*" [ə].

La vocal "schwa" es muy corta y ligera. Los labios deben estar completamente relajados que casi no se muevan al producirla.

202

Posibles Problemas de Pronunciación para Personas de Habla Hispana

En español todas las vocales se pronuncian claramente en las sílabas no acentuadas. La "schwa" [ə] no existe en español. En inglés, las vocales no acentuadas reciben menos fuerza que las vocales no acentuadas en español. Para que los sonidos se oigan como los de alguien nativo del idioma inglés, usted debe opacar cualquier vocal que no esta acentuada en las sílabas de una palabra. *¡La reducción de estas vocales a [ə] no es mala pronunciación sino es lo correcto en el idioma inglés!*

PRONUNCIANDO [aʊ] COMO EN "OUT" (Página 99 en su libro)

LABIOS: se deslisan de una posición abierta a una cerrada y redondeada
QUIJADA: levantada con la lengua y se cierra
LENGUA: se deslisa de baja a alta cerca del techo de la boca

[aʊ] es un diptongo. Comienza con [a] y termina con [ʊ]. [aʊ] se pronuncia de la misma manera que en las letras "au" en español.

Posibles Problemas de Pronunciación para Personas de Habla Hispana

[aʊ] es un sonido familiar en español y no debe presentar ninguna dificultad para usted en inglés. Recuerde que [aʊ] siempre estará representada por la letra "o" sequida de "u" , "w" o "ugh."

EJEMPLOS: ***"out"*** *(afuera)*   ***"cow"*** *(vaca)*   ***"plough"*** *(arado)*

PRONUNCIANDO [aɪ] COMO EN "I" (Página 103 en su libro)

LABIOS: se deslisan de abiertos a levemente apartados
QUIJADA: levantada con la lengua y se cierra
LENGUA: se deslisa de baja a alta cerca del cielo de la boca

[aɪ] es un diptongo. Comienza con [a] y termina con [ɪ]. [aɪ] es pronunciada de la misma forma que en español "ai" o "ay."

Posibles Problemas de Pronunciación para Personas de Habla Hispana

El diptongo [aɪ] debe ser fácil para usted pronunciarlo. Tan solo cuidado con los patrones irregulares de deletreo. Recuerde que [aɪ] puede estar representado por las letras "i" o "y."

EJEMPLOS: ***"ice"*** *(hielo)*   ***"my"*** *(mí)*

PRONUNCIANDO [ɔɪ] COMO EN "OIL" (Página 107 en su libro)

LABIOS: se deslisan de una posición ovalada y tensa a una posición relajada media abierta
QUIJADA: levantada con la lengua y se cierra
LENGUA: se deslisa de una posición baja a una alta cerca del cielo de la boca

[ɔɪ] es un diptongo. Comienza con [ɔ] y termina con [ɪ]. [ɔɪ] se pronuncia de igual manera que las letras "oy" o "oi" en español.

Posibles Problemas de Pronunciación para Personas de Habla Hispana

El diptongo [ɔɪ] no debe presentar ningún problema. Su producción debe ser fácil para usted. Similar al español, las palabras en inglés que tienen este diptongo se escriben con "oy" o "oi." No hay excepciones a esta regla!

INTRODUCCIÓN: ACENTUACIÓN, RITMO, Y ENTONACIÓN

Esta parte del libro que discutirémos a continuación es un poco más difícil de entender que lo que hemos presentado anteriormente. **¡Pero no se preocupe! USTED PUEDE HACERLO!** Tómese su tiempo, escuche las cintas y repase los ejercicios con mucho cuidado.

Hasta ahora, usted ha estado estudiando los sonidos del inglés aisladamente. Estos sonidos (vocales y consonantes) pueden ser afectados marcadamente por caracteristicas vocales conocidas como acentuación, ritmo y entonación. Estas caracteristicas vocales también ayudan a comunicar lo que queremos decir y deben usarse correctamente si usted quiere que se le entienda correctamente.

ACENTUACIÓN es la primera caracteristica vocal que vamos a explicar. Las personas tienen que dar la fuerza correcta a ciertas sílabas en las palabras para ser entendidos. Esta cualidad también existe en español . . . Es a través de esta cualidad que usted puede diferenciar entre papa y papá, seria y sería, o libro y libró. La acentuación también puede cambiar el sentido de una oración: "El **HOMBRE** me habló" es diferente a "El hombre me **HABLÓ." En inglés el uso apropiado de acentuación le ayuda a entender la diferencia entre "present" (regalo) y "present" (presentar).**

RITMO es la segunda caracteristica que presentarémos. El ritmo se crea acentuando fuertemente o rítmicamente la oración. En español, el ritmo se basa en la sílaba. Esto significa que todas las vocales en la sílaba se pronuncian casi iguales. Las sílabas casi nunca se reducen, ni se pierden como en inglés. Por ejemplo, la frase de tres palabras *"Huevos con jamón"* nunca se puede convertir en dos palabras como en inglés *"ham'n eggs."*

Esta reducción resulta porque el ritmo en inglés está basado en tiempo. Esto significa que el ritmo está determinado por el numero de acentuaciones y no por el número de sílabas. Los que hablan el idioma inglés hablan despacio y enfatizan las palabras o sílabas acentuadas. También hablan rápidamente y reducen la acentuación en las no acentuadas. Como por ejemplo con la frase de cinco palabras "I will see you tomorrow" dirían en tres palabras *"I'll seeya t'morrow."*

ENTONACIÓN es la última caracteristica vocal que usted aprenderá. Los patrones de entonación dependen del tono y son los responsables de la melodía del lenguaje o idioma. Las personas cuando comunican dependen mucho de la entonación para transmitir un mensaje. Quizás hasta mas que en la pronunciación de las vocales y consonantes. En español usted puede usar exactamente las mismas palabras para hacer una pregunta como para expresar cualquier otra idea. Si la entonación sube, se entiende que usted está haciendo una pregunta *¿Habla inglés?* Si su voz baja de tono, esto podría significar la expresión de otra idea, *Habla inglés.* Lo mismo ocurre en inglés.

La oración "That's Bill's car" puede invertirse en pregunta "That's Bill's car?" al subir el tono de la voz al final de la oración. Ahora sí puede usted entender el dicho común: **"No es lo que usted dice sino como lo dice!"**

Aunque usted tenga la pronunciación mas correcta usted tendrá un acento extranjero hasta que no tenga el dominio de los patrones de acentuación, ritmo y entonación del idioma inglés.

ACENTO DENTRO DE LA PALABRA

Definición

Acentuación o fuerza se refiere a la cantidad de volumen que se le da a una, sílaba en la palabra. Los sonidos en las sílabas acentuadas son mucho mas largos y altos en volumen que las no acentuadas. Los términos acentuación y fuerza se usan intercambiablemente cuando nos referimos al acento.

Acentuación en Inglés

Una de las caracteristicas más importantes del idioma inglés es el uso de la acentuación o fuerza. Cada palabra de más de una sílaba siempre va a tener una sílaba más acentuada que las otras. Las sílabas acentuadas reciben más fuerza y se oyen más fuerte que las no acentuadas. El uso correcto de la acentuación es esencial para la buena pronunciación en el idioma inglés.

Posibles Problemas para Personas de Habla Hispana

En el idioma español existen reglas específicas de acentuación. Cuando existe una excepción a la regla, el acento se escribe sobre la sílaba acentuada. En inglés no existen reglas específicas. Por consecuencia, usted tendrá dificultad al acentuar palabras en inglés.

EJEMPLO 1:   Usted puede colocar el acento en la sílaba *incorrecta.*

"*désert*" (desierto)   sonaría como "*dessért*" (postre)
"*invalid*" (enfermizo) sonaría como "*invalid*" (nulo)

EJEMPLO 2:   Usted puede enfatizar cada vocal de igual manera y olvidarse de reducir las vocales en las sílabas no acentuadas.

"*tomórrow*" sonaría como "*tómórrów*"
"*becaúse*"   sonaría como "*bécaúse*"

ACENTO DENTRO DE LA ORACIÓN

El Acento Dentro de la Oración en el Idioma Inglés

Usted ya aprendió que una de las características más importantes del idioma inglés es la acentuación de palabras. Los patrones de acentuación van mas allá de las palabras. De igual manera, si suena mal omitir el acento en las palabras, que lo llevan, también suena mal ponerlo en las palabras que no lo llevan. El uso correcto de la acentuación fuerte o débil en las frases y oraciones le ayudarán a que su pronunciación se aproxime mas a la de una persona cuyo idioma nativo es el inglés.

Posibles Problemas para Personas de Habla Hispana

Los patrones de acentuación de oraciones en inglés no se usan de la misma forma que en español. En inglés, las palabras específicas dentro de la oración son acentuadas o dichas de forma mas alta en volumen para distinguirse unas de otras. (*"It's not **HIS** house; it's **HER** house."*) En español usualmente la gramática se aplica de manera diferente para transmitir ese significado. (*"No es la casa de **el**; es la casa de **ella**."*) Eso podría causar problemas si deja de usar el acento fuerte o débil en inglés. El utilizar los patrones del español contribuirá a que su acento extranjero sea más marcado al hablar inglés.

EJEMPLO 1: Usted puede colocar el acento en la palabra errónea. Esto hará que:

    a. su mensaje cambie de significado

       *"He lives in the green **house**"* [El vive en la casa verde] sonaría como *"He lives in the **green**house"* [El vive en el invernadero]

    b. distorsione el significado de su oración

       *"**STEVE'S** my cousin"* [not Sam] sonaría como *"Steve's my **COUSIN**"* [not my brother].

EJEMPLO 2: Usted puede estarle dando mucho o igual acentuación a palabras poco importantes.

       *"I'm in the **HOUSE**"* sonaría como *"I'm **IN THE** house"*
       *"He's at the **STORE**"* sonaría como *"**HE'S AT THE STORE**"*

RITMO

Ritmo en Inglés

Ritmo en el idioma inglés en conversación informal es más rápido y menos preciso que en conversación formal. Toda oración contiene sílabas o palabras que reciben el acento primario. Como en el compás musical, los acentos fuertes ocurren regularmente para crear un ritmo. Algunas palabras dentro de la oración deben ser enfatizadas mientras que otras son dichas rápidamente. Esto hace que los sonidos sean reducidos, cambiados u omitidos. Para mantener la fluidez de la oración, las palabras se agrupan en frases y están separadas por pausas y así transmitimos el mensaje. El uso efectivo del ritmo le ayudará a adquirir una pronunciación natural y clara.

Posibles Problemas para Personas de Habla Hispana

En español, todas las vocales en todas las sílabas se pronuncian casi iguales. Rara vez se reducen las sílabas como en inglés. Es muy posible que usted esté utilizando patrones de ritmo del español cuando habla en inglés y por esa razón su acento extranjero será notable.

EJEMPLO 1: Puede ser que usted acentúe cada palabra de la misma forma o demasiado precisa.

"*He will **leáve** at **thrée***" puede sonar como "***Hé will leáve át thrée.***"

EJEMPLO 2: Puede ser que usted esté evitando usar contracciones o las formas reducidos del inglés.

"***I can't go***" sonaría como "*I **can not** go.*"
"*He likes **ham'n eggs***" sonaría como "*He likes **ham and eggs.***"

EJEMPLO 3: Puede ser que usted esté colocando pausas incorrectamente entre palabras de la oración, que contribuirá a obscurecer el significado y ha crear un ritmo incorrecto.

"***I don't know Joan***" (No conozco a Juana.) sonaría como "***I don't know, Joan***" (No se, Juana.)

ENTONACIÓN

Definición

Entonación se refiere al uso de melodías altas y bajas de la voz al hablar. Todo lenguaje usa tonos bajos y altos y así le da su matiz distinto y entonación diferente. De hecho, los niños recién nacidos reconocen y utilizan la entonación típica de su idioma mucho antes de aprender a pronunciar sonidos y palabras.

Entonación en el Idioma Inglés

A través de la entonación podemos transmitir el mensaje de gramática y la actitud del que habla. La entonación nos dice si la persona está diciendo o preguntando algo. También nos deja saber si está seguro de sí mismo, o inseguro, tímido, molesto o impaciente. Por eso es necesario el uso correcto de la entonación para transmitir mensajes como lo haría una persona nativa del idioma inglés.

Posibles Problemas para Personas de Habla Hispana

¡*Ya usted lleva ventaja!* Debido a que el español tiene básicamente los mismos patrones de entonación que en el inglés. Sin embargo, el inglés tiene más variedad que cambia con el contenido, actitudes y el estado mental. Sin darse cuenta, usted puede confundir a sus oyentes al usar patrones incorrectos de entonación.

EJEMPLO 1: Puede ser que su voz se elevarse cuando debe ser baja en tono. Esto causaría:

    a. un cambio en la oración declarativa a una oración interrogativa o pregunta.

    "That's Bill's car." sonaría como ***"That's Bill's car?"***

    b. que usted se oiga como que tiene dudas o que tiene coraje.

EJEMPLO 2: Puede ser que su voz se quede monótona cuando debe subir o bajar en tono. Esto causaría:

    a. que usted se oiga como aburrido o desinteresado

    b. que usted cause confusión en los oyentes al pensar que usted no ha terminado su oración o pregunta:

    "I went home." sonaría como ***"I went home. . . . . . and. . . . . .***